Chronicles of Micah

REVISED EDITION

War in the Heavenlies

"And there was war in heaven: Michael and his angels fought against the dragon; and the dragon fought and his angels, And prevailed not; neither was their place found any more in heaven. And the great dragon was cast out, that old serpent, called the devil, and satan, which deceiveth the whole world. He was cast out into the earth, and his angels were cast out with him" (Revelation 12:7-9).

A historical fiction of Dr. Yeager's first three months after he became a new creation in Christ Jesus. Names, places, and dates have been changed. Not every situation is an exact retelling of the event.

MICHAEL H. YEAGER,

Chronicles of Micah,
Copyright © 2011 by Dr. Michael H. Yeager

Dedication

This book is written for those who are in pursuit of reality in a world filled with lies. And to our precious little girl, Naomi, who is in the presence of our loving Father. We miss and love you, Naomi, and we are waiting for the day we can hold you once again.

Acknowledgments

Special thanks and love to Kathleen, my closest friend and companion, who also happens to be my wife. Her suggestions and insight were invaluable. To my three sons, Michael, Daniel, Steven, and my daughter Stephanie: words can never describe how precious you are to me!

Contents

Prologue: Heavenly Host

Thunder boomed, lightning flashed, and a multitude of voices singing praises roared like the flood of many rushing waters. Activity was everywhere. Angels ascended and descended to the earth on an invisible super highway, a stairway to heaven. Some of the returning angels brought with them humans that had just passed away, who only moments before breathed their last breath on planet earth. They were the blood-washed redeemed, those who had believed and who had gladly received the free gift of salvation. They had purified themselves with the Word and the Spirit of God, even as Jesus himself is pure. What a blessed homecoming it is for those who had labored in the harvest fields of the world and now were coming home into the joy of their reward and salvation!

Such rejoicing and excitement has never been seen on the earth. There was tearful celebration as the new arrivals reunited with previous acquaintances and loved ones who had gone on before them. Wives hugged former husbands and children greeted their parents. Brothers and sisters in Christ, close friends and companions all reunited after a separation that seemed like an eternity. So was and is the blessed promise of those who believe and live a life of obedience to the Lord Jesus. Heaven is like a huge Grand Central Station, the arrival depot and departing place for angels headed into combat and conflict on the earth.

Many of the angels wear impressive armor, their swords hanging in sheaths at their sides, helmets placed upon their heads or under their arms, and shields swung over their shoulders. There is a constant flow of these angelic warriors. A river of angelic beings heading to and from that little planet where men are born and where men die, the place where human's eternal destiny hangs in the balance and is determined by their own free will.

Chronicles of Micah

Earth is the place where in the spirit-realm battles are being fought continually. There is no such thing as a cease-fire or a truce, for the lives of men, women, girls, and boys of every nation, culture, and language are constantly in the balance.

Some of these angels are the mighty warriors assigned to those who are to be the heirs of salvation. Included in this number are the ministering spirits who take upon the form of natural men. They are sent forth to walk in the midst of humanity fulfilling specific divine missions as the Lord of Host gives them orders. At times they help the desperate by giving encouragement in the time of need or by rescuing those threatened with certain death. Other times they give words of coming destruction so that God's people might escape from certain judgment; just like the two angels that were sent to the Jordan valley to lead Abraham's nephew, Lot, away from the cities of Sodom and Gomorrah, because they were to be destroyed.

These are only a few of the spiritual beings. Each one was created for a specific task. Even as Eloheem created a wide variety of the fowl of the air and fish in the waters, so there is a great variety of heavenly beings, multitudes beyond counting. The Almighty is a God of variety. He takes no pleasure in a production line, cookie-cutter type of operation. Rather, He enjoys variety, diversity, different personalities, and types of life. It is evident that there is no limit to His creativity and ingenuity. It has not even entered into the heart or mind of man that which God has already created or will create in the future for those who love Him. The comprehension of man's limited intelligence cannot grasp the awesomeness of the ability and limitlessness of their Creator.

The relationship that God and His angels have is not one of a dictator with slaves. Rather, their service is one that is performed of their own free will. It is one of absolute love and devotion. The joy and pleasure of their hearts are to fulfill the divine purpose for which they were created. There is no mistake in the fact that the foundation of their devotion is built upon God's love for them. He respects and provides for His creation, like a father does for his children.

Angels are not at all as humans have preconceived them to be. There is definitely no comparing true heavenly beings to cupids—little angels in baby diapers with wings, shooting arrows of love out of tiny bows. This is the image that the adversary of God (the devil) has presented to man in order to belittle those who overcame satan's army and would not follow his perverted mutiny.

In reality, there are many angels that are beyond human description or understanding. Then there are the cherubim, who stand before the presence of the Almighty continually. Their appearance is like that of a man, and their feet are like a calf's. They have four wings, two like those of an eagle on each side, and under their wings are arms and hands like a man. They also have four faces: the face of a man in the front, the face of a lion on the right, the face of an ox on the left, and the face of an eagle in the back. All day and all night they cry, "Holy, holy, holy is the Lord God Almighty."

There are also the mighty seraphim with flaming swords. They are God's divine Green Berets. When Adam and Eve were ushered out of the Garden of Eden because of the seed of sin that had entered their hearts, God placed two seraphim at the gate to keep man from partaking of the Tree of Life, which was in the midst of the garden. If man would have partaken he would have remained in his sinful condition without any possible avenue of redemption like the angels who left their first estate; in which there is no possibility of salvation for them.

Then there are those in charge of the armies of heaven. These are called archangels, the two mightiest of whom are Michael and Gabriel. They are not only in charge over many squadrons of angels, but they are trusted, tried and true servants of the Most High. Michael and Gabriel most certainly proved themselves in the great celestial war in the pre-Adamic time (the luciferian Age) when they boldly stood against lucifer and his damnable mutiny.

The spiritual world is a much superior level of existence than the material realm, just as the material realm is greater than the microscopic world. The fact that the microscopic realm cannot be detected by the natural eye does not in any way prove that it does not exist. Neither does it mean that because you cannot see it, there must be no importance pertaining to it. It is absolutely the contrary. It is proven by the majority of the time, the medical community concentrates its studies to the world that is invisible to the naked human eye. It is a realm that has great negative or positive effects on the health and welfare of the physical part of man.

Likewise in the realm of the spirit, from which all things that exist have their origin, the effects and influences that are exerted upon the physical world by the spiritual are almost unbelievable. There are constant battles and conflicts, head-on collisions of good and evil, that man cannot see. It is a fight and struggle to control the ultimate destiny of the souls of men. While men ignore the existence of these struggles, they themselves are to a great extent a product of these inaudible voices that they harken to—the unseen forces of hell and heaven. To the devil and his forces, men are pawns upon the chessboard of life. But to God, they are precious, valuable souls in need of salvation.

The Spirit of God communicates with man through his conscience. But the satanic world works through the five senses: touch, taste, sight, smell, and hearing, in addition to the intellect of the mind of man which has become darkened.

The angelic realm, the divine guardians of mankind, live and walk in the midst of men, and yet men do not perceive them. Angels are not made of intangible wisps of wind; neither are they the "cotton candy dreams" of little boys and girls. They have spiritual reality, divine substance, operating in the speed of light. Modern scientists in this twenty-first century have proven that if you speed up the molecular structure of solid material to the speed of light, it would cease to exist as man now knows it. You could not see it or touch it, but its substance would be just as real and solid in the spiritual world.

If men and women who believe are kept ignorant of these truths, will not the adversary of their souls lead them down a path of ultimate destruction and death? Should these truths be hidden from those who are called to be vessels of honor, ambassadors of the Most High? Take hold of these realities and enter into the authority that God has preordained for His children to walk in. You shall know the truth, and the truth shall make you free. So let your spiritual eyes be opened, and know without a shadow of a doubt that even now, at this very moment, there is an angel of the Lord standing by your side. A guardian of the Almighty has been sent to protect you. Yes, even you, the reader of this book! Do not think for a moment that you have picked up this book by accident. There is an angel at this very moment watching and protecting you, fighting back the forces of darkness so that you can receive the truths contained herein.

EVIL PERSONIFIED

The satanic world, on the other hand, is composed of the demonic spirits who were formerly angels and disembodied creatures that followed lucifer in his rebellious treason. The spirits of the demonic world are more grotesque and horrible than any mind could possibly conceive. Sin has so distorted and perverted their original natural appearance that there is no resemblance to their original divine glory. A terrible metamorphosis has transpired. The very fiber of their moral character has been totally perverted and demoralized. There remains not even a sliver or spark of repentance. There is no love, mercy, sympathy, or kindness in their bosoms. They are murderers, liars, blasphemers, haters of mankind, propagators of the most horrible and outrageous crimes against creation, against man and God.

Here is a great paradox: When a man who loves God dies, he takes upon himself the absolute, complete characteristics of God: His purity, holiness, righteousness, love, peace, joy, and gentleness. All of God's wonderful and awesome nature is made one with man forever. Never again will that man or woman be tempted, tested, or tried. Forever they will have a perfect love for God, for their fellow man, and creation. Never again will there ever be another selfish act in word, deed, thought, or action.

But when a person dies without making it their ultimate goal in life to love God and has not repented of all known, willful sin, he takes upon himself the total, absolute, and depraved characteristics of the devil. All that satan is, the unregenerate man becomes. All the wickedness, nastiness, immorality, and perversions of lucifer becomes his, and he loses every trait of the divine nature. All that was good and decent is lost forever. Men who die in this state are forever locked up, sealed, and lost in the nature of satan. They are swallowed up in the eternal darkness of complete selfishness.

Many of the fallen angels appear to men as angels of light, so-called "guardians of mystical secrets." They sell their wares to gullible, money-seeking, self-gratifying, power-hungry humans. They appear in many forms promising immortality and limitless authority. They tote lies as the truth, declaring new revelations and higher realms of enlightenment. They push karma and New-Age theologies that deceive men and who have in turn deceived others. Even as the father of lies appeared to Adam and his wife in the garden of Eden, so they follow after the same pattern, promising that which they cannot give because they do not possess it. By their deceptions and perversions, they capture their prey as a spider captures a fly in its web, spinning a cocoon of lies around about their minds and emotions and slowly but surely injecting the deadly venom in order to possess and devour them. Much of their deceptions are woven with biblical truths and principles taken out of context. They teach a Christianity that uses God, instead of one that surrenders its will and life to God. In the garden, satan told Eve that she could eat of the Tree of the Knowledge of good and evil and not die. In the same way, the lie is still being propagated today to the masses of gullible people that we can continue to partake of good and evil and still live and not die. It is a lie that we can be like God and keep living in willful rebellion and disobedience. But true Christianity that brings salvation seeks the perfect will of God and reflects a life that hungers and thirsts after true holiness and righteousness.

These fallen angelic beings have only one purpose of existence, and that is to totally destroy anyone or anything that resembles the splendid nature of the glory of the Creator. They have fallen from their original glory and will never be able to ascend again to that magnificent position. For there is no repentance, nor forgiveness, nor redemption for these pitiful, lowly, corrupted beings that are destined to everlasting torment and damnation in the lake of fire, where the fire is never quenched, and the worm never dies.

Many humans have given heed to their seductive and damnable heresies, refusing to obey God and to turn from their wicked ways.

Instead, they reach and strive for that forbidden fruit that even lucifer grasped for in order to become God, which is the impossible, unattainable, and corrupted dream. For that which is created can never become greater or equal to the One who created him. It is like a gnat endeavoring to become an eagle or the clay pot longing to become the potter. Even as lucifer lusted after God's power, position, anointing and authority, many today who have been deceived into believing that they are Christians are hungering and lusting after the exact same things. In truth, they should be longing for nothing but to be just like Jesus in his character and nature. Through Christ, God has given His sons and daughters the privilege to rule and reign with Him forever.

Chapter 1
Life or Death, Heaven or Hell?

In the heavenly realm Leb'abreck (whose name means, "stout in heart and to kneel"), a guardian angel of the fifth rank, was taking a little rest from his last assignment when his superior, Hodevah (meaning, "praise of Jehovah"), an angel of the Lord, called for him to tell him about his new charge. "Leb'abreck, this will be no easy assignment. The Spirit of the Lord has revealed to the angelic counsel that if this man-child survives and if he submits himself to the will of our Creator, there will be many lives touched and changed by his walk. There is an apostolic call upon his life. There will be many battles and no reinforcements (other angels to help) until he is born anew—that is, if he comes to that place of true repentance, surrender, and obedience to our God," said Hodevah. "It will be one of the most challenging assignments you have so far experienced."

And so from the moment that Micah (a Hebrew name which means,"to be like God") was conceived in his mother's womb, Leb'abreck faithfully began watching, protecting, helping, and ministering to this family. But also from the moment Micah was conceived, the demonic world began trying desperately to terminate him. Of course, this is true of all human beings. There is a battle being fought over their eternal destiny.

Micah's mother had a very difficult pregnancy and despite the best efforts of the doctors to prevent it, she went into labor three months premature. The doctors did everything they could, but Micah's life was hanging on by a thread. Although Micah's mother was not a Christian at the time, she remembered hearing about God as a child. Tears flooding her eyes, she cried out in desperation, "Dear God...if there is a God, You're the only One who can do anything now. God, don't let my baby die. He's so tiny, so helpless, so fragile. I love him, Lord. I want to care for him and to raise him. Let him live. Please…please. I'll dedicate him to your work, oh Lord. Just don't let him die."

Her prayer touched heaven, and the Holy Spirit found a small avenue to keep life alive in his little chest. Yet as Micah grew older, it became evident that the enemy had succeeded in causing him difficult physical disabilities. Bones in his inner ear never formed properly, impairing his hearing. His tongue had grown to the bottom of his mouth, causing a speech impediment, and his lungs were asthmatic, impairing his breathing. The doctors did their best to correct these physical disabilities, but with very little success.

His childhood was not one of enjoyment or pleasure. He had a constant battle with sickness and pain. Because his sinuses were unable to drain, he frequently suffered from severe headaches. It was a continual struggle for him to breathe freely because of asthma. On top of all of this, other children (and later adults) mocked and imitated his slurred speech, constantly ridiculing him. As a child he tried so hard to speak clearly, but he just could not form the words properly and make them come out without being gargled and distorted. Many times he could not understand what was being said to him because of his loss of hearing. This led people to believe he was mentally challenged. He was placed into a special ed class at a young age.

Haunted by his inability to become a normal child and tormented by the ever-present taunts of neighborhood punks, Micah became rebellious and disobedient. By the age of eleven, he had discovered that alcohol seemed to dim the pain that followed him. Not only did liquor pour salve over his wounds, it brought him the one thing he craved—friends. The hoods that once jeered him now took him into their pack.

At age thirteen, he had a very close call with death. While attending a party in an abandoned building located in the city's crumbling warehouse district, Micah "chugged" a third of a quart of vodka. He was so drunk that he thought he was a bird and opened a window on the fifth floor. He proceeded to climb out on the windowsill and prepared to jump. Villainous demons buzzed around his head like flies screaming, "Jump! Jump! Jump!" Leb'abreck scarcely succeeded in getting Micah's best buddy's attention, who came into the room just in time to grab the back of his belt as he began to leap out of the window.

Later that night, at the same party, Micah passed out. While lying on his back, he almost asphyxiated himself in his own vomit. Again, his angel was able to get the attention of another human being, who rolled Micah over on his side. Sadly, however, the young man who saved Micah's life passed out and died a number of years later from asphyxiation. There was no one there to turn him on his side, like he had done for Micah years before. The demonic world has a perverted sense of humor. Unable to kill Micah, the demons attacked his rescuer and killed him using the same gruesome method they tried to use against Micah. He choked to death in his own vomit. His guardian angel was heartbroken, as it is an angel's job to keep their charges from dying and going to hell before they can choose to accept God's plan of salvation, but there is only so much that guardian angels are allowed to do.

Micah's life continued in a downhill spiral. Instead of walking away from the taunting and teasing, Micah learned early on to strike back by fighting. Although he didn't look for fights, he didn't back away from them either; that is how he lost his front tooth and broke his nose three times. When he was old enough to ride a motorcycle, he frequently vented his rage by riding recklessly and at dangerously high speeds. In one of his many accidents, Micah slammed into the side of a tree and broke his nose a fourth time. The only good thing that came out of that accident was that his nose was made a little bit straighter. The dentist repaired the missing tooth with a pegged one; however, the doctors never could take all of the crookedness out of his nose.

Micah became an expert at building walls around himself to hide his true feelings and emotions. He continually drowned himself in alcohol and drugs, trying to forget his past mistakes and failures. His life seemed so useless, so void of purpose. It was filled with vanity, pain, and hurt. He knew in his heart he was living a self-consumed life, but he couldn't seem to stop.

Micah's angel toiled extremely hard to keep him from dying and going to hell. It is a mystery why mortals respond so quickly to the whispers and enticements of demons and rarely ever respond to the gentle, but strong calling of the Holy Ghost. Micah would have been dead many times over if it had not been for the divine interventions of God. Of course, Micah never did give the credit to God, but instead called it luck, like so many other deceived mortals.

In the heavens, Hodevah once again called Leb'abreck, "Tonight is going to be the end of, or a new beginning for, your assignment. For months now, demons have been bombarding Micah with thoughts of suicide, unrelentingly tormenting him. Evil spirits have been constantly at work trying to make him feel inferior because of his hearing disability and speech impediment. He really doesn't have anyone he can call a friend, and most of the people he knows either make fun of him or feel sorry for him. As you know, Micah even dropped out of school at fifteen years old because of this constant ridicule and teasing. Now, on his nineteenth birthday (February 18th), he is approaching the end of the road."

"I know this in my heart," Leb'abreck responded. "I tremble at the thought of his eternal soul being damned forever."

Hodevah continued, "Just this afternoon, Micah purchased a large hunting knife, but as you know, he has not hunted in years. He doesn't even own a gun or a hunting license. If the Almighty does not divinely intervene, Micah will be dead and in hell before morning. Our hands have been tied by the multitude of his sinful, self-centered decisions. Leb'abreck, it is not Eloheem's will that any should perish. But, it is Micah's choice: life or death, heaven or hell. The destiny of his eternity is in his own hands. Nevertheless, you must be ever watchful."

Chapter 2
End of the Road

Standing in front of a mirror in the bathroom of an old, run-down motel room, Micah stared at his appearance. He was not what you would call extraordinary in his appearance or build, there was nothing particularly special about him. At five-foot nine, he weighed 145 pounds and had curly, chestnut-brown hair with hazel eyes that appeared more green than brown. His chest and arms were not extremely muscular, though he did spend a lot of time lifting weights and doing other forms of physical exercise. His face was markedly German with a slightly wide nose and boxed chin. Thick, curly eyebrows framed his eyes, and his hairline had a distinct widow's peak. Micah never shaved his mustache because without it he looked way too young to pass himself off as a twenty-one-year-old, seeing that he was only nineteen.

As he stood there staring, drunk and disoriented, Micah was extremely depressed and unable to think of himself or his life without doubt and criticism. His mind was foggy as to how he even ended up here. He remembered being at some wild party, drunk out of his mind, shouting with his fists flying. He thought that he might have hit someone, at least the torn flesh across his red knuckles made it look that way. Somehow he had managed to get on his motorcycle. He remembered starting the bike, seeing yellow lines twisting and turning, and dark shadows of trees and houses rushing by in a blur. The next thing he knew, Micah woke up in this motel room.

The streetlight shone through the window, striking him full in the face. He waved his hand momentarily to block the rays, then forgot about it. His head was starting to spin a little and the wretched, gritty taste in his mouth made him think that he must have swallowed vomit. He cleared his throat and spit into the stained and grimy sink of the little bathroom. Longing for peace, he closed his eyes for a minute and breathed deeply. Instead, thoughts of Micah's family filled his mind. His older brother was what the drug world called an "acid freak," taking up LSD after it made a comeback in the late 1990s. His sister was into speed and other mind-warping drugs. His father was a hard-working man, trying vainly to provide for his family through a pair of low-paying, menial jobs that constantly kept him away from home. His mother was a loving woman who did everything she could to raise her children properly, but she also worked two jobs while battling her own asthma and sleeping sickness. Micah felt that his family did not care if he lived or died. Of course, they really did care, but it was hard for him to see the truth because he had filled his mind with the lies of the devil. Sin's natural workings have the ability to blind people to the truth, to the future, and to the end results of their sinful lives.

At this moment, Micah had absolutely no spiritual perception that there was a battle raging over his eternal destiny. Unseen by human eyes, the room was filled with demons of suicide. Through the years, other victims had stood in the very room of the rundown motel where he was standing now—struggling and wrestling with an urge to kill themselves. Three of them gave into the demonic urge, and two of them died before medical help could arrive.

Spirits of suicide once again crawled around the room, invisible to Micah's eyes. They were like cockroaches, rats, and silverfish skittering everywhere. An uncanny darkness permeated the room, and even though the lights were on, it still seemed dark and gloomy. In the background, just beyond audible distinction, Micah heard satanic jeers and laughter, mocking, accusing, and belittling him. *You're nothing. Your life is worthless*, the voices mocked. He thought it was just his mind playing tricks on him.

As Micah stood before the mirror, he noticed a bulge under his coat. Unzipping his black leather jacket, he saw the hunting knife he had purchased the day before. He unbuttoned the strap that wrapped around the handle and withdrew it from its sheath. Holding the knife between him and the mirror, he stared at the glimmering steel. Micah placed the sharp blade on his left wrist and began to apply pressure.

Go ahead, the voices urged. *No one will miss you. You'll be better off dead.*

Tears rolled down his face as the hopelessness of his life flooded his mind and emotions. He had failed at everything he had endeavored to do or to be. His whole life was one big disaster, a joke, a worthless use of space and air. As the cold, steel blade began to sink into his flesh, the blood oozed out on both sides of the knife. Micah knew that if he was to succeed, he had to push harder in order to sever the main artery. He remembered a friend of his who once survived an attempt at suicide because the cut wasn't severe enough. In Micah's mind, hundreds of demonic voices screamed, *Do it! Do it! Do it! Now! Now! Now!* He took a deep breath, closed his eyes, gritted his teeth, and then...

Something totally unexpected happened, something strange and definitely supernatural. That little grimy, dirty, cockroach-infested bathroom was suddenly filled with an awesome, overwhelming presence, both extremely terrifying and holy. It was so real that he not only sensed it, but he also physically felt it. It was like an invisible blanket had fallen upon him, enveloping his whole being from head to toe. Time stood still. It was as though a gigantic hand reached into his chest and squeezed his heart.

Light flooded his mind. For the first time in his life, Micah's eyes were opened to see his spiritual condition. Fear—absolute, total holy fear—gripped him. He was lost and undone, separated from God. There was no goodness in him. He was bound for hell. There was no question in his mind whether he deserved it or not, or whether there was such a place. His heart screamed the truth. He deserved hell; he belonged in hell! And hell was opening its mouth wide to receive him. A sinner— that's what he was. He had sinned against heaven and a holy God. He was filthy beyond description; unholy, profane, and rebellious against all that was good or godly. His whole life up to this moment flashed before his eyes. All of the lies, evil thoughts, deceptions, and never-ending list of sins screamed in his mind the reality of his guiltiness. It was overwhelming. Micah was shaking like a leaf in the wind. Before he knew what he was doing, he dropped the knife into the sink and stood in the presence of a holy, righteous, awesome God. He knew that he was in the presence of the Lord.

There was only one other time Micah could remember having experienced a similar sensation. He had been about seven years old. Even during those years, Micah caused his parents all kinds of heartache and sorrow. He was always getting into trouble, yelling, screaming, cursing, and disobeying. He had caused his mother so much heartache. Once, in utter frustration, she told Micah that he had to be the devil himself. She never knew how deeply those words affected her son. No matter how he tried to be good, he just got worse. As a little boy he would get up on the sink in their little bathroom and run his hands through his hair. Under his hands, he was positive that he could feel two large lumps beginning to form on his skull. He was almost positive that he was actually the devil.

On the night of his younger experience, he had gotten up to go to the bathroom. It was a cold, winter night, and there was at least a foot of snow on the ground. The house was very quiet as everyone else in his family was sleeping. As Micah came into the bathroom, the light of the moon was shining through the window. The window was made with milk-colored, perforated glass. As he looked through it, a shiver ran from his head to his feet. For there in the milk-colored glass were three crosses. The middle one seemed to be three-dimensional. An overwhelming sense of love radiated from the middle cross. As he was looking at it intently, he thought there was a figure of a man hanging on it. In his mind, he saw blood flowing from the man's hands and feet. The next thing Micah knew, he was crying—weeping uncontrollably—not understanding what it was all about, yet knowing somehow that God had touched him.

For the next two weeks, the seven-year-old boy was totally different, almost a saint. His parents were amazed at the change that had overtaken him, especially his mother. He was polite, kind, and very helpful. No one had to ask him to help; he simply did it. And even when the other children mocked him, he just ignored them instead of fighting back. He even quit aggravating and teasing his sister. As time went on, however, it wore off. The encounter with God was forgotten as if it had never happened.

Now, here he was, twelve years later, experiencing a sensation that was similar to the one so many years before, but it was so much stronger. Micah walked out of the bathroom and threw himself down on the floor of the motel room right next to the musty, old, queen-size bed. The presence of God was so real he could barely breathe or move. Not knowing what else to do, he began to pray. Of course, he didn't realize it was a prayer. He was simply crying out to the One in whose midst he was. Words flowed from his mouth, torrents of emotions that he had never before experienced. They were totally unexpected and quite strange for Micah, considering that as far as he could remember, no one had ever taught him how to pray, nor had anyone ever witnessed to him about making Jesus the Lord of his life. No one had told him that Jesus was the only way to the heavenly Father or that Jesus gave the supreme sacrifice for man's rebellious and wicked depraved heart. And yet, words flowed from his mouth and Micah heard himself saying, "My God, oh my God, I'm so very sorry. Without realizing it, I have been running from You. I've spit in Your face and ignored You. I thought I could make it on my own. I've messed up my life. Everything I have ever touched or tried to do has gone bad. I realize I am a sinner going to hell. I have sinned against You and heaven. I know now that I cannot make it alone. Jesus, I give You my heart, my soul, my mind, and my body. Change me. Make me a different person. I know You are the Son of God. I believe You died for my sins and that You rose again from the dead. Come into my heart. I am Yours. Take me. Use me for Your glory and honor. I surrender my life to You. I don't want to live this kind of life anymore."

As he finished, something like a bolt of lightning hit him. A supernatural, awesome love began to flow into and roll over him, wave after wave, after glorious wave. In his heart he knew without a shadow of a doubt that God loved him, died for him, rose from the dead, and was coming back. The emptiness that he had experienced and tried to fill with everything the world had to offer—alcohol and drugs, pornography and sex, fast cars and sports, materialism and money—was now filled with an eternal quality called the presence of God.

As the burden of his past was lifted off of him, Micah laughed and cried, shouted and danced with joy. Suddenly, Micah felt he had discovered the true purpose of his life, and a strong desire rose up on the inside of him to go and tell others about what God had just done. He now knew that almost everyone he had ever known was not right with God. Even as he had been lost because of his wickedness, so they were also lost and damned unless they would believe on Jesus and give themselves totally over to Him.

Chapter 3
The Battle Begins

The regions of darkness boiled over with hate. Belee (corruption), one of the ruling demons in sector five, screamed murderously, "What have you done? How could you allow him to escape? You told me he was already in our hands, that even by tonight he would be ushered into eternal darkness. You guaranteed his death."

The lesser demons cringed in total terror and confusion. Shaking with fear, they could only utter whines and gurgling sounds.

"Answer me, you useless fools, before I rip you apart limb from limb," screeched Belee.

One of the unclean spirits, Rah (mischief, wicked, trouble) spoke up with a high, screechy voice that sounded like fingernails on a chalkboard. "Your most powerful, we would have had him. The knife blade was moving toward his wrist. We saw his life force begin to flow out of him. His mind and emotions were under our control. It was so close, and we were moving in for the kill. The mortal's guardian angel just stood back, rendered helpless by this fool's free will. Then, all of a sudden, a bright light flooded the room. There was an explosion that threw us head over heels out of the building. We tried to re-enter, but a multitude of angelic beings surrounded the motel. We stormed them again and again, but their numbers were too great. Many of our battalion were wounded and are not yet fully recovered."

Belee screamed, "Shut up you worthless, ugly, good-for-nothing imbecile! Don't you talk about such things around me." As he screamed, his already hideous face became twisted and distorted with unimaginable hatred. "All I know is that you were told to kill this miserable human being. And what happened? You not only failed in this simple task, but you also allowed him to go to the other side. For nineteen years we have worked to destroy him, plotting, conniving, and planning his death. We almost had his miserable mother kill him in the womb. We had her convinced that all there was within her was a blob of flesh and that it would not be a baby until it was brought forth, but you allowed some fanatical religious nurse to get to her."

Belee continued, "I should have never given you all of those chances. Now, not only is he alive, but he is also a believer! He is a walking time bomb. If he ever discovers who it is that now lives within him, and what He has made available to him, I can absolutely guarantee that not only are your heads going to roll but mine will also. If Kosmo Kraton, the high prince of our sector, finds out, we will experience pain and torment a thousand-fold greater than we have ever experienced up to this moment. Do you realize and understand the full implications of what has happened? This Micah has the potential of changing the whole course of history. From the beginning our adversary has had him marked for a vessel of deliverance, to pull down our strongholds. Multitudes and multitudes could be delivered from our clutches. A virtual domino effect could transpire. We have seen this happen too many times before. All of our work will be wasted and ruined because of your stupidity. Time is running out. We must not give our opposition any more vessels to be used against us."

While the satanic world screamed with hatred and dismay, the heavenly realm rejoiced with the sounding of angelic trumpets, singing, shouting, and dancing. Heavenly beings from the least to the greatest celebrated—angels and archangels, seraphims and cherubims, saints who had gone on before. Creation itself was exuberant at the prospect of having given birth to a new son of God.

The Most High had declared that a regenerated, spiritually resurrected, born-again man was worth more than all the wealth of the world. Jesus said a single born-again soul is like a pearl of great price, the coin that had been lost, or the buried treasure in the field. So valuable was man's redemption to God that He had even given Himself for man's redemption. Man was not valuable because of his own self-worth, but simply because God had established his value in the spiritual market. God plants the incorruptible seed of His divine DNA and nature into the soil of the souls of willing men and women, in order to re-create His image in the heart of the human race.

Leb'abreck was overwhelmed with joy. The last nineteen years had not been in vain. The enemy had not succeeded after all. Micah was in the arms of God, spiritually speaking that is. He was now a child of the King—an heir and joint heir of Christ. The process of his transformation had begun, though there would be many trials and tests before the full manifestation of an apostolic anointing rested upon him.

Leb'abreck was not only excited about Micah's conversion, but also the fact that he would no longer be alone in his endeavor to protect and minister to Micah. Other guardian angels were on their way to assist him. When a human being is conceived in their mother's womb, they are assigned an angel; but when a person accepts Christ, other angels are assigned with the first one, because angels of the Lord encamp around about them that fear Him.

"Hail, Leb'abreck, in the name of the Lord of Hosts. Truly with great joy we have been sent to assist you and to minister to Micah, this new son of our Lord. We have no time to waste. We have just received word that our adversary is already mounting an attack on Micah. They want to reclaim the territory they have lost, so we must speedily get to his side and use all of our heavenly abilities to protect and help him."

Five muscular, angelic warriors, Tabeal (God is good), Tsaphah (watchman), Nay-fo (sober and calm), Sawkal (prudent and prosperous), and Leb'abreck streaked through the heavens toward a corrupted and polluted, obscure little planet called earth. With shear determination on their faces, they drew their swords. As they passed by the stars in the heavens, their sword blades flashed with brilliant, blinding light. The battle was just beginning. There was no doubt that a fierce battle would unfold before the day was over.

Chapter 4
New Experiences

Three days had come and gone since Micah had repented of his sins and had given Christ his heart. His whole being was totally transformed. There was no comparison between who he had been and who he was now. Joy and peace radiated from him like a neon light. In zeal, he was like a living tornado. Wherever he went, he shared what happened to him. He just could not tell enough people. He longed to be just like Jesus and have others be like Him, too.

As Micah drove down the road on his motorcycle, he saw one of his old drinking buddies, Larry Johnson. Pulling off to the side of the road, he turned off his bike and parked it. "Yo, Larry," Micah called out. "Come here, I've got to talk to you."

Larry was a tall, husky young man. He had tattoos up and down his arms like Chinese writing. He wore five earrings in his left ear, and his hair was bleached in the middle of his head, making it look like a racing stripe.

"Oh yeah, what's up?" asked Larry. As Larry approached Micah, he could see that there was definitely something different about him. "Hey, Micah you got some new stuff? The way your face is shining, you must really have a buzz."

"No," said Micah, "I have something that is much better than dope. What I've got you never have to come down from. It's out of this world. And it's not some kind of artificial or chemically-induced happiness. It's the real thing, man."

"Okay, I'm curious," replied Larry. "What is it that you have?"

"It's pure and simple," answered Micah. "I have Jesus! Or maybe I should say, Jesus has me!"

"You what?" Larry almost shouted back.

"I've met Jesus, Larry. He's for real. Three days ago I was at an old, cockroach-infested motel. You know, one of those dumps we usually crash in. I was trying to commit suicide when a bright light suddenly flooded the room. You probably won't believe this, but it came from heaven."

"You have got to be out of your mind," Larry responded.

"Look at me, Larry. Do I look like I am out of my mind?" Micah asked. "I'm telling you, Larry, it's for real."

For the next thirty minutes, Micah expounded on what had happened to him and how this experience with Jesus had totally transformed his life. Before Micah had finished, tears were flowing down Larry's face.

"What's happening to me?" whispered Larry.

"That's the Holy Spirit," said Micah. "God is here right now, Larry. God is here to set you free from the lies of the devil, and from what the Bible calls the sinful nature, just like He set me free. He cares deeply about you, Larry. Jesus came and died so that you can live forever."

The conviction of God was so heavy upon Larry he could barely talk. Larry whispered with a reverential voice, "Micah, what do I have to do to get right with God?"

"First," said Micah, "you have to mean it with all of your heart."

"I've never been more serious in all of my life," replied Larry.

Micah and Larry prayed together right there on the side of the road. Afterward, Larry shouted, "I'm free, I'm free. Hey man, I am free." His face radiated pure joy.

What happened to Larry was typical of what happened wherever Micah went. And the more people responded, the bolder Micah became. Boldness, like a mighty trumpet, rose up within Micah as he declared how God had set him free. He was no longer in bondage to drugs, alcohol, or cigarettes, and his mind was no longer filled with pornography and violence. God had set him free from his greatest enemy—himself. He had quit these addictive habits because he did not need or want them anymore. He knew he had become what the Bible calls a new creation in Christ because he was changed on the inside. He didn't have to work hard to be good; the goodness of God on the inside of him had changed his desires so that he wanted no part of darkness and sin anymore. But he didn't understand why this time was different from previous church experiences.

He didn't have to wait long, however, to get an answer. One day something happened beyond Micah's wildest imagination. He walked up to a total stranger who looked to be in his thirties, and he began to share his experience. "Praise God," the man shouted. "I've already got what you are talking about. I gave my heart to Jesus three years ago, and instantly my whole life was transformed. My name is Lester. What's yours?"

"It's Micah."

"Micah, I'd like to talk with you some more. How about a cup of coffee?" Lester asked.

"Sure," Micah said.

While drinking their coffee, Lester began sharing some biblical truths that Micah had never heard. He could hardly believe what he was hearing. How could it get any better than it already was? Micah thought back upon his religious upbringing. He had hated going to church, all of those people who acted like saints on Sunday and then lived like the devil the rest of the week. Plus, it was boring, dead, and dry. The pastors never truly taught that when man disobeyed in the garden, he lost the image of God. They never trained anyone that when man no longer loved God, he no longer loved holiness, righteousness, purity, or obedience. They never taught that the heart of man had become altogether corrupted, wicked and deceitful above all things, just like the devil. They never told you what was really involved in true conversion or salvation, that in order to be saved God would have to give you a new heart, a new way, and a new spirit. "Religion tries to change man from the outside in," Lester explained, "but Jesus changes man from the inside out."

Micah said, "I never liked church because I always felt I could never be good enough like the church said I had to be."

Lester explained, "It's like this. You can cut all of the branches from off the tree, and yet the root system is still there. These branches could be drugs, alcohol, adultery, pornography, and all kinds of sin. Religion goes for the branches. But Christ goes for the root, which is the heart. That is why John the Baptist said that the ax must be taken to the root of the tree. The truth is what sets you free, not man-made rules and regulations." It's the spirit of Jesus Christ inside of you.

Micah shared with Lester some of the bad experiences he had in church when he was very young. "Some ministers always seemed to be talking about money, teaching people how they could get more from God, as if he were a cow to be milked, or some kind of celestial Santa Claus. And some of the preachers claimed that healing and miracles are things God used to do but didn't do anymore."

Lester nodded. "Yeah, I heard some preachers say that God is totally unpredictable. He might give you cancer or kill you in a car accident. Then when stuff like that happens they say, 'God is in control.'"

"When I was little I decided that if Christianity was really like what a lot of these preachers preached, I didn't want anything to do with it," Micah said. "And that's why I never had anything to do with church, right up until I tried to commit suicide."

Lester continued to share how God is a good God. "The Bible says, 'Beloved, I wish above all things that you might prosper and be in health, even as your soul prospers.' Does that sound like an unpredictable God who wants you to be sick, broke, and defeated?" Lester asked.

Micah thought about what Lester was sharing with him. All his life he had seen God as some ogre in the sky waiting to pounce on him and pronounce judgment for the slightest infraction of the rules. Now, here was this stranger telling him the total opposite of what he had heard all of his life. "Lester, if what you're saying is true," said Micah, "how come I never hear preachers telling it that way?"

"To be honest with you, Micah, I think it is because they have never been taught right. They are not teaching what they learned from the Bible, but instead they are teaching their denomination and religious upbringing. If they would simply go to the book of Acts, they could see for themselves how the church, or you could say the body of Christ, is supposed to be, but they have been blinded by lying spirits. You see, Micah, there is a spiritual world. Right now, at this very moment, there are angels of God right here with us. They hear everything we are saying right now. They are protecting and watching over us to help us as God directs them. But, there is also a satanic world. Jesus said the thief cometh not but to steal, to kill, and to destroy, but that Jesus came to give us life, and that more abundantly. The angelic world and demonic forces are constantly doing battle for the souls of men, including ours. Satan and all of his forces are out to steal every heart away from loving God and to destroy the character of God in man. The life that Jesus came to give us is the character and the nature of His Father developed and manifested in the believer's heart."

Lester continued, "For instance, if you'll read the Scriptures, you'll see that Jesus healed everybody who came to Him in faith believing. According to Acts 10:38, sick people are all oppressed of the devil, but God anointed Jesus with the Holy Ghost to heal them. Jesus is the same yesterday, today, and tomorrow. It's God's will that everyone would repent, be saved and healed so that they would live a holy, separated, zealous life for God."

"You mean," Micah said, "that God would heal me of my hearing disability and speech impediment?"

"According to the Bible, He will. That is, if you have truly repented and turned from your sins." Lester pulled out a small pocket-sized New Testament. "Let's just see what God's Word says about healing." For over forty minutes they searched the Scriptures together, looking at Isaiah 53:4,5 Matthew 10:1, Mark 16:18, Luke 4:18, 1 Peter 2:24, and Malachi 4:2.

"Well, Micah, what do you think?" Lester asked.

"I never knew that was in the Bible," Micah replied.

"Yeah, a lot of people don't. Micah, have you ever been baptized in the Holy Ghost?" Lester asked.

"I have never even heard of the baptism," responded Micah. "What is it?"

"I think I have covered too much ground already. I'll tell you what. You go home, get your Bible out, and look up everything you can find in the Bible on the Holy Ghost and healing, and we'll get together another time." Lester gave Micah his telephone number and address, and Micah put the piece of paper in the pocket of his black leather jacket. "By the way, where do you go to church?" Lester asked.

"Do I need to go somewhere to church?" asked Micah.

'Sure you do. God's Word says that we should not forsake the assembling of ourselves together with the saints. Besides, what are you going to do with all of those new believers? You need to be fed spiritually by the apostle, prophet, evangelist, pastor, and teacher. It will make you more effective for God," Lester replied.

"Yeah, I guess you're right," Micah responded. "Thanks Lester, I'll start looking. "Don't forget, call me any time," said Lester as they parted company

Micah rushed home. As soon as he entered his apartment, he pulled out his Bible and a *Strong's Exhaustive Concordance*, which he had recently purchased at a local Christian bookstore. For the next two days, Micah poured over the Scriptures. It was a real eye-opening experience. The more he read, the hungrier he became. It was amazing to him how there could be so much available to a believer, and yet so few know what is already theirs because of Christ.

At the end of the second day, Micah got down on his knees next to his bed and prayed, *Lord, I believe. I choose to believe what Your Word declares. Your Word says that only a faith that works by love, which produces obedience and holiness, pleases You. My body, my head, and my five senses declare that it just can't be, but I choose to believe You. You bought me with Your precious blood. You delivered me from the wrath to come. If I can trust You for my eternity, I am going to trust You for my here and now. Lord, You said You would send the Comforter to teach, to guide, to convict us of our sins, and to empower us. I need the Holy Ghost to be a witness and to move in supernatural gifts that You might be glorified in and through my life. Father, I ask You, in the name of Jesus, to baptize me right now in the Holy Ghost and power.*

At that very moment, the presence of God entered the room. A strange, warm tingling feeling filled Micah from the top of his head to the bottom of his feet. Then something began to happen in his belly; it was like a bubbling in his innermost being. His mouth began to quiver. The next thing Micah knew, he was speaking in a beautiful foreign language. All of the things that he had ever wanted to say and express to God, but did not have the words to say, were flowing from his lips. It was just like in the book of Acts on the day of Pentecost! For how long Micah prayed in this heavenly language, he did not know. The glory of the Lord engulfed him. It seemed like time itself no longer existed.

The next morning Micah woke up feeling tremendously refreshed and spiritually strong. Radiating with the presence of God, he took a quick shower, dressed, read his Bible, prayed for a while, and ate his breakfast. Then, he put on his coat and prepared to go to work. As he stepped out into the brisk morning air, he saw one of his next-door neighbors. It was Mrs. Denton. He had grown up with her three sons, Mitch, Darrel, and Craig.

"Good morning, Mrs. Denton," said Micah as he walked on the sidewalk toward the road. "How are you doing this beautiful morning?" asked Micah.

"Why, Micah, what has happened to you?" she responded with absolute surprise in her voice.

For a moment Micah was taken back. "Mrs. Denton, can you really tell that I have changed?"

"Well, yes, it is quite obvious if you ask me," she replied.

"Mrs. Denton, I gave my heart to Jesus, and now my whole life is radically changed." Micah thought she was talking about his conversion.

"Well, Micah, I think that is wonderful, and I am very happy for you. But that is not what I am referring to," answered Mrs. Denton. "For the first time in fourteen years, I can understand exactly what you are saying!"

It was true. God had performed a marvelous miracle for Micah. When the Holy Ghost came upon Micah and gave him utterance in a new language, He also took away his speech impediment. As the reality of what God had done dawned on him, he began shouting his gratitude from the depths of his heart, "Thank you, Jesus! Glory to God! Hallelujah!" Those who saw or heard Micah shout probably thought he had lost his mind, but that didn't bother him in the least. God had done for Micah in one moment what the modern medical world could not do for him in nineteen years of operations and speech-therapy classes.

Micah had been on fire before, but now he was ablaze. Everywhere he went, he shouted out the great things God had done for him. As the word began to spread, Micah became the center of talk at the factory where he worked, the clubs where he used to dance, and the motorcycle gang he used to hang out with. The "word" was out that he had lost his mind and that he had utterly lost touch with reality.

Chronicles of Micah

They thought he had become some kind of space cadet or a crispy critter. Fear gripped their hearts when his name was brought up. It was not a fear of physical harm, but an uneasy feeling of some type of coming judgment. A divine fear was beginning to descend upon this average modern-day, sinful community.

Chapter 5
The Clash of Titans

In the spirit realm, trumpets sounded in the night as the heavenly host shouted words of battle and encouragement to one another. As thunder echoed over the valley of death, Leb'abreck and Hodevah watched as the clashing of swords in the supernatural world sent sparks flying into the darkness. Shields rang as they repelled the weapons of another. Screams of pain and agony roared out as arrows found their marks. Limbs that were severed lay scattered across the battlefield—writhing, jerking, twisting, refusing to die—waiting to be retrieved by their owners. As Leb'abreck gazed across the scene before him, Hodevah mused, *Two forces—spiritual armies in deadly conflict—fighting over potential treasure and wealth greater than gold or silver, far beyond the value of land or material possessions.*

On one side were heavenly-looking beings. Their features would dazzle earthlings if they could be seen. Angels are strapping brutes with bulging muscles and perfectly chiseled features. They look like men in appearance, but not as man is known on planet earth. To this day, no artist has ever come close to painting a mortal as awesome as those who fight in this valley. In the past, when humans have come into contact with the heavenly race, they have mistaken angels as gods, sometimes falling down to worship them.

Not all angels look the same in feature or size, and even some of their armor is different. Their weapons vary from swords, to spears, to bows with fiery arrows that look like lightning bolts when fired. Some are foot soldiers marching to the instructions of others, and some ride creatures beyond earthly description. Although somewhat frightening in appearance, angels are definitely mighty in battle and terrifying in their swiftness. Some ride in chariots that appear to be on fire, yet they do not burn and they are not injured. Harnessed to these chariots of fire are huge, horse-looking creatures. They are not horses as humans know them, because fire proceeds from their nostrils, and they can take to the air like eagles while pulling the chariot and its occupant with almost no strain. They dart here and there with the light-footedness of a gazelle and rush headlong into enemy ranks, wreaking havoc wherever they make contact.

The angels who remain now chose to serve their Maker during the luciferian age. Though the lies had been extremely clever and deceptive, two-thirds of the heavenly host refused to believe the accusations lucifer made against their Lord. But sad to say, one-third chose to believe the liar and followed him in his conquest to overthrow God. So the celestial war was started.

The battle is never ending. At times, these battles have been known to rage for more than twenty-one days. Fresh angelic beings come and replace those who are wounded or weary. These are pure, holy beings in combat against insane, sinful, and self-loving, demented creatures.

Leb'abreck turned to Hodevah and said, "These evil, wicked beings are not dumb beasts, but conniving, plotting, rebellious aliens who have invaded the earth."

"Yes," Hodevah answered, "They have come to steal, to kill, and to destroy. They have come to rule, to reign, and to turn men into slaves of perverted and disgusting desires. Their strength is not that of the heavenly hosts, but they make up for it with their deceptions and guile. These creatures, destined for hell, have no mercy. They are twice dead, filthy dreamers. They despise divine dominion, and are like clouds without water. There is no room for repentance in them, for they are rotten to the very core. The Prophet Jude wrote about them. The angelic warriors, on the other hand, fight with dignity, honor, and mercy, but these devils of hell know no such code of ethics. Whatever it takes is their modus operandi."

Ugly is not a sufficient word to describe the appearance or character of the demons, yet there are those within their ranks who disguise themselves as angels of light. Outwardly, they are beautiful and deceptively so; inwardly, they lust, murder, and are wicked beyond the imagination. Theirs is a world of hate, lies, and perversion.

Hodevah looked thoughtful as he contemplated the state of humanity. "The majority of mankind has seemingly always been more willing to believe their lies instead of the eternal truth. They have given up their lives by the billions for fleeting, momentary pleasures. They look for that elusive pot of gold at the end of the imaginary rainbow. They are ever striving, but they are never able to experience the fullness of life as God has ordained. Instead, they follow after the promises of the great pretender—he who promises that which he can never deliver or fulfill. The one who was once called lucifer relies totally on mankind's evil nature and gullibility in order to manipulate them."

Leb'abreck nodded agreement. "And it has come to pass that this present generation of men is more possessed of evil spirits than any previous generation. They have opened their minds to these spirits through deceptive New-Age doctrines, politically-correct thinking, secular media, modern education, and the entertainment world."

"Yes, it's sad, " Hodevah responded. "Modern Christianity, which is nothing more than mere humanism in disguise, teaches that the most important thing in life is one's own personal happiness. Now more than ever, the forces of hell are mounting aggressive attacks in order to drive all heavenly presence away from dying humanity."

Hodevah sighed as he continued, "For thousands and thousands of years there have been battles between these forces: good against evil, light against darkness, selflessness against selfishness, right against wrong, and love against hate. Many times it looked like good was defeated by evil, but good always triumphed at the last moment. Wherever men have submitted themselves to that which is right and holy, the forces of heaven move in power and authority."

Leb'abreck commented, "When lucifer rose up against God, he never imagined that God or the angels who had remained faithful to him would put up a fight. All the angelic host had ever seen of God was the divine attributes of his goodness."

"That's true," Hodevah said. "Creation itself had revealed and expressed nothing but his kindness, gentleness and meekness. God had never had an occasion to express His holy wrath and anger, indignation and tribulation. But then it was too late. The devil and all of the rebel spirits that followed him then knew that their final destiny was hell."

"The modern-day church has fallen into the same snare and lie to a great extent," Leb'abreck said. "All that they talk about is God's goodness, mercy, love, and forgiveness, never realizing that all who refuse to repent of their known and willful sins will experience God's judgment and anger."

Hodevah agreed. "Men now have an opportunity given to them that the angels which lost their first estate never had and never will have. Man can repent and be converted. But most of humanity have refused to turn from their wicked ways, not looking to Christ for the victory to overcome their fallen nature and to come out of their wicked lives. Sad to say, they will end up in hell with the devil and his angels."

"You'd think they would learn," Leb'abreck said. "Now it has been two thousand years since Christ ascended to His Father, and instead of the battles ceasing, they are growing in magnitude and violence. It is like one last great effort to finish off what has been going on for generations beyond count: the consummation of all things."

"There can only be one victor, for both cannot survive or exist together," Hodevah said. "One of them must be eliminated and only one will be left to rule and to reign."

Chapter 6
The Promise

Micah was sitting in his small apartment with his bare feet propped up on a footstool that was made out of a tree trunk he had cut with a chain saw. He was reading the Bible and listening to worship music on his MP3 player. He had recently downloaded three Christian albums from the internet after trashing all of his secular, worldly music. Through the Bible, Micah had discovered that he could not please God and grow spiritually by continuing to fill his mind with the trash and perversion of the world. The Scriptures that he found very clearly declared, both in the Old Testament and the New Testament, what kind of life God now expected him to live—a life that is holy, pure, and given over to nothing but God.

He was totally absorbed in the content of Isaiah chapter 53. The sidenotes in his Bible said that Isaiah was a prophet and that he wrote these Scriptures eight hundred years before Christ came to earth, and yet the picture it painted was explicit about what happened to Jesus. The pain, sufferings, and agony described therein were graphic and horrible.

"Father God," Micah whispered, "I never realized what Jesus went through for me. I did not know that they had beaten His body until you could not tell He was a man." Large tears formed in his eyes and rolled down his cheeks as the realization of what Christ had done became apparent to him.

On his lap was a piece of paper with several other verses written down that he was studying: 1 Peter 2:24; John 19:1-5; Acts 10:38; 1 John 3:8; James 5:14. Basically, the only truth Micah had ever heard previously was that Jesus died for his sins. He had never been taught that Christ came to give people a new heart, one that loves all that God is and hates more than anything the evil that is contrary to the will and the character of His Creator. Neither had he been taught about the thirty-nine stripes that Jesus had received upon His back, or that the Roman's whip actually tore flesh and muscle off with each stroke due to the pieces of glass, bone, and steel fastened to the end of the leather straps. When Pilate had declared, "Behold the man," he presented to them a man who had been ripped to shreds with blood flowing from head to toe, wearing a crown of thorns with spikes over two inches long buried into His skull. His face was a mass of quivering, open flesh where they had torn His beard out. Micah thought to himself, *this could not have been the work of just men, but it had to have been work inspired of demons.* It became apparent to Micah why Jesus had gone through what He did. Faith rose like a mighty giant in his heart.

"Lord Jesus," Micah spoke out loud, "You did it for me, to deliver me, to heal me, to set me free. By Your stripes we were healed. If we *were* healed, then *I was*, and if *I was*, then *I am*. I AM HEALED!" Micah shouted.

Even though Micah was born again, he still had a lot of physical problems. Since birth, his hearing was extremely bad. He was also allergic to dust, which would occasionally cause his lungs to fill up to the point where he could not breathe, and he would end up in a hospital spending weeks at a time in an oxygen tent. His sense of smell was almost gone, since his nose had been broken at least four times, once in a motorcycle accident and three other times in bar fights.

As he sat in his chair, he found himself speaking to his physical infirmities. Micah did not know why he was doing it, he just sensed that it was the right thing to do as authority and power flowed from his lips. "In the name of Jesus Christ of Nazareth, I speak to my sense of smell, and I command it to be normal. And in the name of Jesus, I command this allergy to go. In the name of Jesus Christ of Nazareth, I command my ears to become normal right now. I said, now, in the name of Jesus Christ of Nazareth!"

It was not as if he were commanding God to do anything. He was simply operating upon the premises that his physical body is the temple of the Holy Ghost. And if Christ went through all that suffering and pain to make him whole, it would be a sin not to appropriate his healing.

His words hung in the air. The atmosphere tingled with tangible authority and power. Instantly, Micah's ears popped open. The music that he was listening to became so loud he could not stand it. He ran for his stereo system and turned it down. It was then that he noticed a foul smell that was absolutely putrid. He began to look around, trying to locate it. Then it struck him. The smell wasn't something in the room; it was coming from him. More specifically, it was his feet. They stank so bad it almost made him choke! He ran for the bathroom and filled the sink with hot water and soap. Then he stuck one foot in the sink and washed it, took that one out, and stuck the next one in.

For nineteen years he had suffered with some of these ailments, and now in less than the time it takes to tell the story, God had totally healed him, simply by his knowing the truth, believing the truth, and acting upon what the Bible said. This was not at all the Christianity Micah had been brought up with. The Christianity—or the religion—that Micah knew as a child was dead and boring. It consisted of going to church every Sunday, singing some old, dry songs, and hearing a preacher give a fifteen-minute speech. Micah could not have even told anyone what the message was about because the preacher never said anything that held his interest. Very rarely did the minister speak from the Bible. It was usually a newspaper clipping or a journal from a psychologist or New-Age psycho-analyst.

But what really discouraged Micah the most were the people. In church and around the preacher they were so pious, holy, and righteous. But Micah knew better because he had seen them away from that environment. They were anything but godly. They cheated, lied, swore and told filthy jokes. They were gossipers, tattlers, drunkards, and adulterers. You name it, and that crowd was involved in it. And yet, if you had asked them if they were ready to meet their Maker, they would have declared unequivocally, yes. Not only were they worldly, but they were also defeated. They had no true spiritual joy, no peace, and no victory. They were always physically and emotionally sick, and had spent more of their time going to doctors, psychologists, hypnotists, and New-Age psychoanalysts than they had ever spent reading the Bible or doing the work of the kingdom. In fact, if the preacher ever mentioned the need for more help or that the church needed money for a project, they would act just like a crowd of hyenas. The government-run health care, welfare, and job programs had turned them into nothing but takers. They didn't know how to give or how to be aggressive in their commitment to God. They really did not know what it meant to love God. Micah realized that he had not really been better than any of those people he had known. They were all deceived into believing that they were right with God and that they were all going to heaven no matter how they lived.

These apparent contradictions and lack of power in Micah's religious upbringing had driven him away from God. Unfortunately, this didn't happen only to Micah, but it happens to many just like him every day. People that are really hungry for God go to church to find Him. But sometimes all they really find is religiosity. It is a form of godliness, but it does not have any power to overcome the world, the flesh, or the devil. Yet now, here he was experiencing primitive New Testament Christianity, just like in the book of Acts—alive and powerful. All of these years he had been taught by the religious crowd that you could not overcome sin and that healing, miracles, and the supernatural had all passed away when the last apostle died. But Micah had discovered in the Word that this was an absolute lie. Jesus Christ was and is the same yesterday, today, and forever. It was this same Jesus who had set him free from his former life and had healed his body.

Soon after this miraculous healing, Micah discovered in the Bible that it was God's will for him to find a good Bible-believing church. Lester had encouraged him to find a body of believers, and yet Micah needed to see it in the Word of God for himself, because it was a bit difficult for him to accept this as God's will. After all his bad experiences in church as a child. And it was not easy either as there were very few churches in this twenty-first century that really believed and taught what the Bible says. Micah had discovered that many churches had strange, weird doctrines like, for instance, that God makes you sick to teach you things, or that accidents and tragedies are instigated of the Lord, and that all religions lead to God, or everyone needs a spirit guide. Micah was sure these had to be doctrines of demons. There were also those who believed that in order to be saved all you had to do was pray a magical little prayer of asking Jesus into your heart, even though there was no desire to be free from sin or any true hunger for God's divine nature.

One day, when Micah walked into a church; the congregation was singing robustly. He immediately felt the presence of the Lord as he entered the sanctuary. People had their hands lifted in the air. Some were crying, others praying, and the altar was full of people seeking God.

The minister, Raymond Morris, began to speak. He was a middle-aged man of medium height. The only thing he held in his hand was the Bible. As he opened his mouth, the authority of God flowed from him. He definitely was very different from the preachers Micah had known as a child. Pastor Morris was delivering a powerful message about loving God with all of your heart, soul, mind, and strength. He said, "This is the ultimate purpose in life for every believer. If we truly love God we will obey His Commandments. We will be just like Jesus in purpose and nature and we will have a passion to seek to save those who are lost."

It seemed to Micah that he had finally found a place he could call home. In addition, it also turned out to be the church where Lester attended. At the end of the service, Lester walked up to Micah. "Hey Micah, I'm glad you came."

"So am I," responded Micah.

"Come with me, and I will introduce you to our pastor," said Lester.

Micah and Pastor Ray hit it off right away. The pastor even loaned some of his favorite books to him in order to help him grow. They were books about men such as John Wesley, Charles Spurgeon, John Bunyan, Ashel Nettleton, John G. Lake, Charles Finney, and Smith Wigglesworth. Micah was anxious to read these books and to find out about others who had experienced the deep moving of God upon their lives.

Week after week, Micah attended Life in Christ Victory Center and grew in strength and wisdom. The atmosphere of worship and the Word of God were causing him to become solid and stable in his faith and to understand divine biblical principles. God began to move upon Micah's heart to become more involved. One day he went to the janitor and asked if he could help in any way. Micah could see there was a lot that needed to be done. This was no little one-room church; it was a large complex. There was always something going on, whether it was their radio station, TV ministry, discipleship classes, the food and clothing pantry, or the Christian school. Their Christian school had grown quite large since the federal government had totally taken over control of the public school system at the turn of the century. When the public schools began introducing all kinds of bizarre philosophy and immoral teaching, there was a mass exodus out of the public schools and into the private Christian schools. This not only took place with Christian families, but also with families that had even the slightest degree of common sense.

Before Micah knew what was happening, he found himself mopping the floors, cutting grass, helping with the children's church, and cleaning toilets. When Micah wasn't at his secular job or seeking God by praying, reading, or witnessing, he was at the church helping with whatever needed to be done. His heart was to serve the Lord in whatever capacity he could. There was no job too menial. *If Jesus could humble Himself to be obedient unto death, then surely I could become a servant*, Micah thought.

He also began attending home-based Bible studies that the church had established. One night, Micah went to the home of one of the church's elders who was also a home group leader. After the Bible study and time of prayer, something unusual happened. As he stood in the front room of the house simply looking around, out of the blue a man, whom Micah did not know, seemed to stand out. As Micah looked at him, an image and a word seemed to float up into his mind. The image was that of a bulge, and the word was *hernia*. Micah, not being a doctor or even being familiar with medical terms, did not know what it meant. He stood there trying to ignore it, but it just became stronger on the inside of him.

He prayed silently to the Lord, *Father God, if You want me to go to that brother, I will. But I don't know what to do. Please show me, Lord.*

Not two minutes after Micah prayed this same man walked up to him. "Hi, my name is Frank," he said to Micah. "First time I've seen you here." They carried on casual conversation for a little while until finally Micah could not stand it any longer. "Frank, I don't want you to think I am strange or flaky. But before you came over to me, I believe that God was speaking to me about you."

"He was? What did He say?" asked Frank.

"Well, it's not like He actually spoke, but it's more like He showed me something."

"What was it?" asked Frank.

"Do you have a hernia?"

How did you know?" Frank replied with surprise in his voice.

"I believe the Holy Spirit showed me," replied Micah.

"I have had nothing but problems with it. Three times now they have gone in and sewed it up, but my stomach lining just keeps tearing," he explained .

"Can I pray for you?" asked Micah.

"Yes, please do," Frank replied.

Micah laid his hands upon Frank's stomach. He could actually feel a large bulge. He began praying, "Father, I thank You in the name of Jesus for revealing my brother's need. Lord, I don't believe You told me just to tell me, but You told me in order that You could heal Frank. Now I take authority over the works of the devil, and in the name of Jesus, I command you, devil, to loose my brother right now. I speak to the hernia and I command it to go. In the name of Jesus, be healed, Frank."

At that very moment, Micah's hand moved. The bulge literally leaped backwards and was gone. Frank began to shout and cry at the same time, "I'm healed! I'm healed! Thank You Jesus, I'm healed!"

Micah and Frank praised God together for what had just happened. Those gathered at the home group asked what the commotion was about. Frank shared with them what the Lord had just done for him and how God had used Micah to bring it to pass. The whole home group exploded in rejoicing and praising God.

While the church was rejoicing, however, evil was plotting. In the corner of the room stood a pretty, young, blonde woman named Stacy Smith. She was the daughter of the elder whose house they were meeting in. Her attention was solely upon Micah. Her light green eyes twinkled with an unspoken thought.

Chapter 7
Evil Conniving

In the spirit realm, demonic imps—messengers of satan—circled overhead like a flock of buzzards. Invisible and silent, but extremely dangerous, they were looking, watching, and waiting for the right moment, longing to steal, to murder, and to destroy. Unclean perverted spirits with uncontrollable lust; these spirits of pride and deception were wicked beyond all imagination. They were looking for a habitation—a warm body to dwell in. They were like parasites draining their victim of all its life, until the poor soul died, forever damned. Then the search would begin all over again. Blood suckers, leeches, and spiritual tapeworms; that's what they are and of the worst kind.

At this very moment, a small number of them hovered above Micah's head. Every once in a while one would dive down straight for Micah's head, but instead of penetrating, the imp would bounce off like a ball hitting a concrete wall. They tried every entrance imaginable, but there seemed to be no way to enter in.

As they continued to hover over Micah, like flies around a horse's back, they discussed their situation with each other. "What are we going to do?" screeched Aw-ran (whose name means, "curse, bitterly"), one of the lesser imps. "This despicable human is becoming stronger every day. He is so dogmatically one-track minded that we can't even get his attention. All he ever does is pray and speak those disgusting, blasphemous words. How can Belee expect us to stop him?"

Even as they reasoned among themselves, another devilish imp, Fob-os (meaning, "put in fear"), showed up with a message. "You are required to go immediately to see Belee," squeaked the newcomer. The imps trembled as they were summoned. When they finally arrived, they could sense trouble in the air. They fell down at Belee's ugly, three-toed feet. "Yes, your mightiness," screeched Ponos (which means, "great trouble"), the imp who had been in charge of the expedition.

Belee was breathing heavy and shaking with rage from head to toe. "What's going on?" he screamed. His voice echoed off the cavern walls. "I've heard nothing but bad reports. How come you haven't stopped this Micah? He's making havoc in the northeast quadrant. He is just a stupid, ignorant, young baby Christianite. You worthless bunch of unproductive rejects. I want this Micah stopped. I don't care what it takes. If the powers that be get wind of this, there's going to be some heads rolling, and mine won't be one of them."

"Bu-but, y-y-you don't understand," screeched Ponos. "We've done our best...uh, I mean our worst. He keeps coming back at us with these powerful words. We don't understand how he learned to use the Word so effectively. We have attacked much older Christians, even so-called "big preachers," and we've had little opposition. But this character is constantly slamming us with these unspeakable words. Many of our battalion have been put out of commission for weeks at a time. Every time he opens his mouth, he rips some of my troops apart. We don't think he even realizes the damage he is doing to us. Even his angel has not done as much damage as he has with his disgusting mouth."

"I don't want to hear any more of your excuses, and exaggerations" hissed Belee. "All I know is that he has got to be stopped. Enough is enough." As Belee ranted and raved, a thick, sticky darkness descended upon him and the other demon imps. It wasn't just darkness, but an indescribable stink so rotten and putrid that Belee and his imps began to gag, choke, and even vomit because of its fumes.

A voice spoke out of the darkness, like the sound of ripping steel. As Belee heard the voice, he shook uncontrollably. "Belee," the voice screeched. It was Raw-ah (meaning, "to afflict, to hurt") the terrible.

"Yes, yes your power," Belee stuttered.

"Why have you failed me?" asked Raw-ah, his voice echoing from the darkness with a deep grinding sound.

"How have I failed you, your power?"

"Don't act stupid with me. I know all about this Micah. Do you think what he's doing has gone unnoticed. Already he has destroyed

47

years of conniving and plotting. It is sending shock waves through my domain. This is your only warning. If he causes any more problems, it will be your head. I'll skin the hide off of your ugly personage. You have not even dreamed in your worst nightmares what I'll have done to you."

"But your power, we have done everything within our limited influence to stop him. Every day we attack him, trying to find his weak spots. If we could hit him with something that is way beyond his knowledge, I think we could seriously damage his faith in you know who?"

"Well, what do you suggest?" growled Raw-ah out of the darkness.

"I need more help," answered Belee, "one who is much greater in wickedness than he is in his walk of faith." There was silence for what seemed to be a long time. Belee knew better than to say anything more.

"Very well," replied Raw-ah. "I have one who has been successfully possessed and taken over by a number of ruling spirits. Surely he will not be able to stand against this one. He's totally under our control. If need be, we can even have him murder this fanatic."

Fiendish laughter reverberated throughout the cavern. Human ears have never heard such wickedness. It was beyond earthly description. Even Belee and the imps covered their ears with their claw-like hands.

Chapter 8
The Challenge

As the days turned into weeks, and the weeks into months, Micah was constantly in the Word, praying, meditating, and sharing Christ. Many of his old friends accepted the Lord, and he tried to disciple them the best he knew how. He took them to church, baptized them in water, taught them the truths of God's Word, and prayed for them. Once a week, he even had a small gathering at his apartment for those he was trying to reach for Christ. Of course, this was with the permission of the pastor and under the encouragement of Lester.

One night, Micah was sharing the gospel with three of his old friends, Bobby, Willy Whine, and Hasson. He had been witnessing to them for a number of weeks, and this was the first time he had succeeded in getting them to come to his apartment since he had been born anew. As he was showing them verses in the Bible, there was a loud knock on his door. When Micah opened the door, a young, strange-looking man was standing on his steps.

"Can I help you?" said Micah to the stranger.

"I heard you were having a religious meeting here tonight."

"That's not exactly true," replied Micah. "I am having a small get together to share the truth of God's Word." Micah did not want to sound ignorant, but he sensed something definitely weird and unholy about this guy.

"Well, my name is Tee Jay, and I was sent to shut your rotten, no good, filthy mouth." Before Micah knew what happened, Tee Jay pushed his way past him and into his apartment.

"Hey man, you can't do that," protested Micah.

Tee Jay kept walking, totally ignoring everything Micah was saying. He entered the small front room where the other three men were

49

gathered. Walking to the center of the room, he spread his legs in a defiant, fighting manner and declared with authority, "I am here to tell you that my master's not going to put up with your preaching anymore."

"Well, just who is this master you're talking about?" asked Micah.

"My master is lucifer, son of the morning," Tee Jay sneered. As soon as he said this, an invisible presence entered the room. A feeling of impending disaster—a heavy, dark evil—enveloped the whole apartment. From then on, it was hard to keep track of what took place. Micah's mind went numb. The next thing he knew, Tee Jay was standing up on his log-tree footstool. Foul, evil words flowed from his mouth like a city sewage pipe. There definitely was a supernatural satanic power and ability being demonstrated in him. He boasted about a coven of demon worshipers that he belonged to, and he described the way they killed innocent girls and children in their satanic rituals. Holding up his hands, he showed where the ends of four of his fingers had been severed; he said that he had eaten them for power.

Bobby and Willy Whine were glued to their chairs. Their eyes and ears were focused on the center of the room, where Tee Jay was waving his arms like a windmill. Tee Jay was totally possessed by some kind of evil spirits. The other young man, Hassan, grabbed his jacket and ran out of the apartment without saying a word.

Micah did not know what to do. He had never dealt with someone who was full of demons. He knew that something had to be done and that he could not allow this to go on. He prayed silently to the Lord, and as he did, a thought came to him to call Lester. He went to his kitchen, grabbed the phone, and dialed Lester's number. For a while it looked like no one was there to answer, but right before he was about to give up, the LCD screen lit up and Lester's face appeared.

"Hello, Micah, sorry it took me so long, but I always check out who is calling on the secured video channel before I answer."

"Thank God you're home," responded Micah. "I really am in need of a miracle."

"What are you talking about?" asked Lester.

Micah explained to him what was taking place. "Can you come over and help me?" asked Micah.

"I don't know Micah. It sounds like it's out of my arena."

"Oh, come on Lester, I need your help," Micah pleaded.

"Well, I guess so; I'll be right over. But I am not promising you anything. It will take me about twenty minutes to get over there, so hold on."

From the time Micah hung up the phone until Lester arrived seemed like an eternity, even though it was probably less than twenty minutes. When Lester knocked on the door, no one answered. Lester opened the door and stepped inside very cautiously.

Lester had been a Spirit-baptized believer for three years, but he had never personally dealt with a demon-possessed person. He had seen them in the streets as this was a day and age where many were inviting spirit guides (demons in disguise) to take over their lives, but he had always avoided them. Now he was heading right into the midst of that which he dreaded the most.

The minute Lester entered the apartment, an eerie, dark feeling flooded his being. It was dark in the entryway, but this was a darkness beyond the ordinary. Lester tried to reason with himself that because it was late at night, the natural darkness of the hour probably just made it seem spooky. As he stood there, he heard voices coming around the corner. He walked down the short hall and around the corner. He could see the glow of a dim light coming from underneath a door. He moved closer to the door, put his hand upon the door handle, and slowly turned the knob. He cracked the door open very slowly.

As he entered the room, his eyes fastened upon a strange-looking young man in the center of the room, standing on a log. As Lester looked at him, Tee Jay's eyes burned with a reddish glow. His voice was the strangest, though. The voice didn't even sound like it was coming from him. It was an ear-piercing, grinding-type of voice, and the vocabulary that was coming from his mouth was blasphemous in character. He was mocking God, His Word, and Micah. He was declaring that lucifer was mightier and superior to the Lord of Host. He was like a raving madman bragging about the works and wonders of his master.

Just about then, Micah looked up from where he was sitting and there stood Lester just beyond Tee Jay. Relief flooded Micah's face. But just as quick as Micah spotted Lester, Lester spun around and darted for the door. Micah jumped up and ran after him as fast as he could. When he finally caught up to him, Lester was already getting into his car.

"Hey, Lester wait a minute. Where are you going? I need your help." Micah had stepped in underneath the gull-wing door of the car. It was one of the newer models that was powered by hydrogen.

Lester's countenance was one of fear and confusion. "I'm sorry Micah. I just can't help. That is one messed-up character. It's out of my league. He must be full of unclean, New-Age spirits."

"Come on Lester, you can't leave me with this guy. I have two other unbelievers in there that don't know the Lord."

"I am sorry, Micah, but I can't help."

"But you're the one who told me about the Holy Ghost and the authority we have in Christ," replied Micah.

"I know," answered Lester, "but this is too much for me. I wouldn't be in faith, and you don't need me around operating in fear. For some reason, I perceive that God has a plan for you to set him free. You're going to have to pray and get the mind of Christ." And with that, Lester started his car with a whir, put it in drive, and pulled away from the curb, closing the gull-wing door in the process.

As Micah stood there watching the car drive away, he experienced something that would happen many times to him in the future. It was a feeling of absolute inadequacy. In the past, Micah had gone through self-improvement classes that taught a philosophy of having a good self-image and believing in yourself. He was taught that he, himself, was the only god that he would ever need. But he could never seem to convince himself that it was nothing more than a mind trip. It never did away with his speech impediment, or the pain that gnawed away at his heart, or his guilt for the sins he had committed. It was not the good self-image philosophy that had brought him to a place of repentance and salvation. No, it was quite the opposite. It was the realization that without Christ, he was lost and undone, a sinner forever separated from God. He was like a lump of clay without the skillful hands of the potter; nothing but a heap of slimy mud until the potter worked it, molded it, shaped it, and fired it through the furnace of life. Only then could it became a usable and valuable vessel, a vessel of honor, sanctified and fit for the Master's use.

As Micah stood there, he looked up into the stars. What he saw was not the signs of astrology or the Zodiac, but the beautiful handiwork of an awesome, loving and caring God. To think that the God who created those heavens was not only his Creator, but He was also his Father. The thought overwhelmed him. It filled him with a strength and boldness beyond himself. He turned and faced his apartment, straightened his shoulders, and walked briskly back up the sidewalk. As he went through the door, not only was the feeling of evil still there, but there was also a terrible stink. It was the foulest smell Micah had ever smelled. It was so bad that he could hardly breathe. As his eyes adjusted to the darkened room, he could see his two remaining guests still frozen to their seats with absolute terror etched on their faces.

Then there was Tee Jay. A wicked power, a gross darkness, had totally overtaken him. He was laughing with a voice that was beyond description. It was eerie, high, and without question, demonic. Two eyes glared out of his face, gleaming with a red, devilish glow. In his right hand he clutched a knife. When Tee Jay spotted Micah, he began to scream. "I am going to kill you, you cursed, God-loving Jesus freak." With that he let loose of a long line of unspeakable curse words.

Micah should have quaked with fear and should have been absolutely disgusted at the sight of this young man possessed by demons, but instead, out of his innermost being, he felt a divine, supernatural love rise up inside of him. He fell to his knees and began weeping, not just for Tee Jay but for his other guests as well. "Oh, Father God," cried Micah looking up toward heaven. "I don't know what to do, but these men came to hear about Your goodness, Your love, and Your faithfulness. Lord, You're greater than any of this devilish activity. Exalt Yourself in the midst of this attack. Set Tee Jay free from the bondage and sin he is in."

As Micah prayed, a pure, bright light shined right down through the ceiling of that apartment. It totally engulfed him. Whether or not anyone else could see it, Micah did not know. He had a sensation of someone standing right behind him. The overwhelming impression caused the hairs on his neck and arms to stand straight up on end. The next thing he knew, someone's hand was on his right shoulder. He could not see it, but it was there all the same.

In his heart, Micah knew it was the hand of Jesus, and that supernatural, divine strength and power were flooding his whole being like a lightning bolt of sheer heavenly energy. It burst forth out of his mouth like a nuclear explosion. In just a matter of seconds, the whole room was filled with the glory of the Lord. Conviction of the Holy Ghost filled every crevice. Micah's two original guests lay on their faces, weeping and asking God for forgiveness.

Tee Jay was on the floor wriggling like a giant snake. Micah stood over the squirming, demon-possessed man. With a voice of authority, he spoke to the spirits inhabiting Tee Jay. "You foul, unclean spirits, I command you in the name of Jesus Christ of Nazareth, come out!"

The minute that these words came out of Micah's mouth, a voice in a foreign language came screaming out. The spirit tore through Tee Jay as he left. But that was not the end, because another came out in like manner, then another, and then another. At least five different voices in different languages came screaming out. Tee Jay collapsed into a deep slumber. Micah wondered if he was dead, but he knew better.

Everything in the room had grown totally quiet. The two guests were sitting on the floor with tears flowing down their cheeks and their faces glowing with joy, for they had come to know Jesus in that moment when God's manifested presence had filled the room. The peace of God had moved in the midst of their little gathering. It was like a gentle winter snow, enveloping, covering, embracing, and comforting them.

After a while, Tee Jay began to stir. Slowly, he sat up. "What happened to me?" he asked. "Where am I and how did I get here?"

"Tee Jay, Jesus just broke the power of the devil over your life and set you free," Micah said softly.

Tee Jay looked back at him in astonishment. Then tears began to flow down Tee Jay's face. He tried to wipe them away, but as he did, more tears replaced the ones he wiped. "I really don't understand what you're talking about, but I know in my heart it's true," said Tee Jay. "I feel so clean and pure inside. I've never felt this good."

"That's Jesus, said Micah. "He has cleansed you, but now you must allow Him to fill that emptiness with Himself before those demons come back and you become seven times worse."

"What do I have to do?" asked Tee Jay.

"You have to believe in the Lord Jesus with all of your heart and confess Him as the Lord of your life with your mouth." Micah shared with him all that the Lord required. Right then and there Tee Jay opened up his heart, and he was gloriously born anew and filled with the Holy Ghost.

It was not an easy road for Tee Jay. The enemy does not allow his captives to go free that easy. But by God's grace and with the help of the brethren, Tee Jay grew in the wisdom, power, and knowledge of God. Tee Jay went from that place like a sledgehammer in the Lord's hand. Lying demons had deceived him, but by God's grace, he was determined to declare the truth and to set others free. He was glorious in boldness, and he realized that the Lord had a divine plan for his life. Wherever he went he preached Christ crucified.

Chapter 9
Boiling Rage

Ear-piercing screams escaped the mouths of the imps as they experienced unbelievable torment and horrifying pain. They flew through the air, head over heels as their legs and arms flung from here to there. Demons smashed against cavern walls like rag dolls tossed to and fro in a tornado. Unrelenting agony was being dished out with no restraint. They pleaded, whimpered, and begged; all to no avail. Their cries of mercy were totally ignored. Embers of absolute sickening hatred had been stirred and nothing was going to abate it. The dark powers of hell were boiling with rage. A rampage of anger and resentment flowed like a river of sewage. It was a tidal wave of nauseating iniquity.

"This upstart of a Christianite, Micah by name, will pay for his meddling intrusions," bellowed an earth shaking, rumbling voice. (Christianite was what the demonic world called true disciples of Christ.) "He has stolen one of our prime inhabitants. It took years to deceive and beguile him, plus he was leading many others down the same path of destruction with him. He was a chalice we could not afford to lose, and now he is gone, lost, ruined, and destroyed. He is not fit to live any more. What is going to happen to those who followed him? By all that is wicked and ungodly, I'll have this Micah's head if it is the last thing I do. I'll put an end to him. We will stomp his miserable carcass into the ground. We will get him just like we got others like him through the years."

"Belee," screamed Raw-ah, "where are you, you worthless idiot, you son of perverts?"

A squeaky, whimpering voice that was hidden in the darkness finally spoke up, "I'm, I'm here, Raw-ah, my lord."

"Come here. Now!" demanded Raw-ah. "It is your fault! How come you haven't put a stop to this nonsense? You told me you had it under control. Enough is enough. Put an end to him. There has got to be a weak link, a temptation, a twisted, perverted, thirsting lust in his life that will bring about his downfall. There has to be a part of his fallen nature, some type of sin that he has not yet crucified."

"Your power," screeched Belee, who was still racked with pain from the bashing he had received from his superior. "The angels of the Almighty are encamped around about him. We haven't been able to penetrate their fortification. They can't stop us from tempting him, but we can't kill him. And every time we do tempt him, he speaks that powerful Word. We would rather face your wrath than the eternal Word. It penetrates us right to our innermost being. It rips, tears, and engulfs us with fear of God's coming judgment."

"You weak, sniveling coward. No wonder we lost in the pre-Adamic war. It is because of those like you that we have been humiliated, cast out of the heavenlies, and defeated. You're not worth the pain I have inflicted upon you," bellowed Raw-ah.

"But your power, you know what happened. It wasn't our fault we lost the chalice. We couldn't stand against the power that is in that name. Why, not even the prince of darkness himself was able to defeat Him in His death."

At this statement, the corners of the deep seemed to go into convulsions. Belee fell to the ground with a painful moan, and the floor of the cavern cracked open. Fire engulfed him. He screamed as the wrenching agony of pain emanated from his burning figure.

"Please no, no, no, stop," Belee pleaded. The bone-crackling, hideous voice of Raw-ah came back. "Don't ever let such words proceed from your mouth. There is no power in heaven and earth like our master. Is he not the father of lies? Is he not the author of murder? Do not the weak pay homage, bowing to his every deception? Those who were made in the image of God—they have become our offspring and our slaves. Not only our slaves, but also our habitation. We live in them, we think through them, and we do the works of our master through them. Is not lucifer the god of this world? Even God's own servants acknowledge this in their writings. We are not yet defeated. Every day we become stronger. Wickedness is engulfing this world at an all-consuming rate.

And once we have completely captured the heart and mind of this race, we will launch out from this planet and take over all of creation. We may have lost the original rebellion, but we will not lose the last and final war."

Raw-ah continued, "And this Micah is no match for what I have planned for him. There is a chink in his armor, a weakness, a sinful, perverted and twisted fleshly desire, and we will find it. And when we do, he'll curse the day he was ever born." A sickening laughter bounced and reverberated off of the walls of the deep. "And as for his so-called converts, we will give them more hell and misery than they have ever thought possible. They will wish to their God that they had never been saved. And as for Tee Jay, I myself will pay a little visit to him. And when I do, that will be the end of his miserable existence.

Chapter 10
The Attack

Micah was ministering to Tee Jay on a daily basis by praying with him and by teaching him what truths he had come to experience. Tee Jay was becoming a powerful tool to help share Christ with others, and yet he was under constant attack by the demonic forces that had inhabited him for so many years. The battle was becoming so intense that Micah invited Tee Jay to stay at his apartment for a short period until the adversary was sent fleeing.

One night as Micah was sleeping, he woke with a start. Something was wrong. A tangible evilness permeated the room. As he looked over to where Tee Jay was sleeping on the floor, he noticed that Tee Jay was sitting up. There was just enough light coming through the window that Micah could see that Tee Jay's face was petrified with fear. Tee Jay mumbled, "He is here to kill me, he is here to kill me..."

For a moment, fear gripped Micah; the hair on the back of his neck and forearms stood straight up. Micah slowly turned his head in the direction Tee Jay was looking, and then, Micah saw it: a shadow on the wall. It was not an ordinary shadow, but a demonic figure, the form of a large man with what seemed to be reptilian wings and two horns growing out of his head. The shadow stood still, but its chest rose and fell like that of a breathing being. Its wings slowly folded and unfolded.

Before Micah could respond, a voice seemed to come out of nowhere. "You cannot escape me. You have sold your soul to my domain. It is I who am your master," said a voice that sounded like steel being ripped in two.

Tee Jay started to scream as the shadow moved toward him. As Micah gazed at the scene unfolding before him, something stirred within him. It was more than just boldness; it was a divine holy anger. The next thing Micah did was without natural thought. The Spirit of God came upon him. He leaped out of his bed and automatically set his feet in a spread position, like a man who has just drawn a two-edged sword and is ready to fight to his death. The two-edged sword came forth out of Micah's mouth. He heard the words and the voice, but he did not really comprehend what was being said out of his mouth. His voice sounded with total authority; his words were those of one who must be obeyed. "You foul unclean spirit of deception, you have no authority here. No longer do you lay claim to this man, for the blood of Christ has ransomed his soul. He has been delivered from your power and has been translated into the kingdom of God's dear Son. So I command you, in the name of Jesus Christ of Nazareth, and by HIS BLOOD go from him now."

As Micah spoke these words, the shadow appeared as though it had come in contact with another unseen force. It struggled and fought to no avail. Tremors seemingly hit it and shook it, starting with its chest and moving to its head and to its feet. Micah, in his imagination, could almost visualize an angelic warrior with a broad, two-edged sword in his hand. He could see the sword slicing through demonic, reptile-like flesh.

High-pitched, eerie screams filled the air. Wind, like that which would be created by the flapping of huge wings, flooded the room. The demonic shadow went into convulsions; pain racked its image. Then it quivered from its feet to its head one last time and dissolved through the apartment wall.

The minute the shadow disappeared, all fear and satanic intimidation was gone and was replaced by an awesome feeling of peace and joy. Tee Jay shouted with excitement, "I am free, I am free. Glory to God, he's gone for good. I know it. I know it in my heart. Praise God. Thank you, Jesus!"

Micah joined Tee Jay's praises. Together they celebrated and thanked God for the authority granted to them in the name of Jesus. They rejoiced that in His name no demon of hell could stop them, and that at the mention of that name, every knee must bow and every tongue must confess that Jesus Christ is Lord!

Chapter 11
Coming Battle

All of the angels were ecstatic, exuberant, and overjoyed. None of them had ever thought that Micah would yield his life to the Holy Ghost. They never dreamed that he would become such a potent weapon in the hands of the Almighty. Leb'abreck rejoiced to be a part of Micah's life.

Guarding Micah was no easy job. With each success Micah had, there was always retaliation from the demonic world. Wherever Micah went, a spiritual battle was fought, and he was constantly in the middle of the war zone. More and more angels were summoned to withstand the onslaught of the adversary. The demonic powers were bent on Micah's destruction, and not only his destruction but also the destruction of all of those who know the truth, proclaim the Word boldly, and strive to live a holy and righteous life in Christ Jesus. The demonic world aggressively opposes those whose only purpose in life is to love, serve, follow, and obey God.

In the heavenlies, Leb'abreck recounted the battle to Hodevah. "Never do I remember there being a day such as this," Hodevah responded. "The final curtain is being drawn to a close. Evil powers are absolutely frantic, like sharks when they smell blood in the water. The atmosphere is charged with the coming battle, the battle that will end all battles."

He continued, "The world of flesh and blood is totally ignorant, or should I say blind, to the immense warfare that is taking place around them. It is not a battle over land or physical wealth, but it is a battle for the most valuable and precious item ever conceived or created: the pearl of great price, a treasure hidden in the field. It is regenerated, reborn, converted mankind—those who are taking upon themselves the image and likeness of God. You see, Leb'abreck, the value of one converted human soul is worth more than all the wealth of the world. That is why

61

Jesus our Lord was willing to pay the ultimate sacrifice with his own blood, to redeem mankind from their lost and fallen state."

Leb'abreck contemplated Hodevah's words as he thought about the spiritual battles being fought in the spirit realm, the conflict between good and evil, angelic and demonic. He said to Hodevah, "Most humans do not understand what happens, because it is invisible to their natural eyes. Yet, it is not an imaginary fight or just mind against mind. There is literal contact. Humans do not realize that we are tangible, living beings that extricate limbs and spiritual muscles; supernatural beings that groan and moan while we wrestle flesh against flesh. Sparks fly from our spiritual swords, as the sound of battle echoes throughout the chasms of the invisible world. Pain and agony are afflicted upon both sides. We cannot die, but we do experience immense pain. We inflict wounds upon each other. We subdue and are subdued; we torment and overcome. Our recovery from battle wounds is quite extraordinary, yet we are wounded."

Gregoreuo (which means, "watch, be vigilant"), one of the principal angels in the host of the army, approached Leb'abrack. He was a large angel, over ten-feet tall, with angelic white wings folded behind his muscular back. A short battle sword was strapped to his side, and on his breastplate the image of a lion protruded. Under the feet of the lion were red, fiery, serpent-like dragons. As he came closer, Leb'abreck stood to attention and saluted him with a heavenly salute. Gregoreuo returned the salute and stated, "Leb'abreck, we have word from on high that your charge, Micah, is going to have a visitation from the Holy Ghost. We also have word that the adversary is getting ready to mount a fierce attack."

"You must have your squadron on alert." Gregoreuo continued, "The enemy is actively seeking a way to destroy Micah, or at least a way to distract him from the Lord. If the adversary can capture his attention or heart with some temptation, the Holy Ghost will not be able to enlighten him. It is of the utmost importance that the hunger of God keeps burning in his heart."

Leb'abreck responded, "How many have we seen like Micah, who began to move in the authority and power of Elohim and then someone or something came along and stole away their love for God and their commitment. We cannot prevent the enemy from tempting him. Neither can we control his free will, but we can and must strengthen his inner man."

Gregoreuo continued, "Two more warriors have been assigned to your troop. They are champions from the pre-Adamic celestial war. Their names are Gil-bore (meaning, 'mighty, valiant') and Saw-on (which means, 'warrior, to trample'), and they are mighty warriors. From now on, they will be under your charge. The Lord has granted unto them the right to carry a flaming sword like those used to guard the gateway to Eden."

Leb'abreck asked, stupefied, "But Gregoreuo! Is this human of that much importance? The flaming swords are only used in the most serious circumstances."

"I do not question my superiors," declared Gregoreuo. "I simply listen and obey." And with that he turned and walked briskly away. He had other orders he must give and carry out.

Leb'abreck also proceeded to give out directions to his troop, in order to prepare them for the coming battle. "It will take all of our skill and strength to withstand this onslaught of the enemy. At this moment, all is peace and quiet. After every encounter with the enemy, there is a short period of peace, but after the quiet comes the storm. So, be ready."

Chapter 12
Test of Love

As usual, Micah was at church early. He always tried to arrive before anyone else so he could pray and also see if the pastor needed any help. He desired to be a servant, and it did not matter if anybody recognized him or not. He was not doing it for man's approval but because he was consumed with the love of Christ. Besides, Micah reasoned that it was not just the janitor's job to straighten the chairs, empty the garbage, and scrub the toilets; it was the job of all of those who had a heart to serve. And the janitor could always use extra help anyway.

While Micah was picking up old bulletins in the sanctuary, a very attractive young lady walked up behind him. "Hi," came her sweet, melodious voice.

Caught totally by surprise, Micah jumped. The young lady giggled at him. "Uh, Oh, I'm sorry, I didn't know someone was here with me," stuttered Micah.

"Oh, that's okay, I was just watching you," she said sweetly. "You're Micah aren't you?"

"Yes, how did you know?" replied Micah.

"One of my friends told me your name. I've been, you might say, curious about you ever since you started coming here."

"You have?" said Micah, with a note of surprise in his voice.

"Sure. I think a lot of the congregation is curious about you. It seems like every week you bring new people, and some rather strange ones, too, I might add. Oh, by the way, my name is Malinda Harmon."

"Nice to meet you," said Micah. Not knowing what else to say he just stood there. He found himself unconsciously staring at Malinda. She was a beautiful young woman with long-flowing red hair and large, almost hypnotic, turquoise eyes. It was enough to make any young man shiver. She was probably about five-foot-seven with a slender build, but not what you might call skinny. She was quite attractive, and she knew it, too. She relished Micah's stare.

"Would you like to go out with me tomorrow night?" she asked with a very seductive voice.

"What?" Micah was taken back by surprise. He wasn't used to a Christian girl being so aggressive.

"I said, would you like to go out with me tomorrow night?"

"Where are you going?" Micah asked hesitantly.

"I'm going to a dance, and I need a partner. I'd really like it if you would take me."

"You're going to a what?" Micah asked, once again in disbelief.

"A dance. It's just a little party some of my friends are going to have. It's really going to be fun." As she said this, she moved closer to him, until they were almost touching one another. Micah's hands grew sweaty.

"Thanks, Malinda, but I don't think so," responded Micah, his voice trembling as he spoke.

"Aw, why not Micah? I am sure we'll have a real good time."

"I am a Christian, Malinda."

"Well, I am, too," answered Malinda in a voice that wasn't so sweet. "But I don't think the Lord minds us having a little fun. We're only human, you know. I even saw a bumper sticker the other day that said 'Christians aren't perfect, we're just forgiven.' Come on, Micah. Don't be such a square."

"No, thank you, Malinda," Micah said, backing away from her.

"Why not?" Malinda asked..

Micah drew a deep breath and said, "Because Jesus gave his life so that I do not have to be a slave to sin anymore. I used to live a self-consumed life. I was sick in my heart and my mind. I tried all that the world had to offer me—the drugs, the illicit sex, the alcohol, fast cars and all of the other sick, wicked and perverted things. Jesus delivered me from that foolishness. I had more than my fill of it all before I gave my heart to Christ. It definitely did not please God. And to be quite honest, it's quite boring compared to the true workings of God. Now if you want to pray, pass out tracts, memorize some Scriptures or go witnessing, I would love to do that."

Malinda was shocked. She had never, in all of her memory, ever been turned down. Most boys came on to her quite aggressively. As a matter of fact, this was the first time that she had ever been so outspoken to a boy, and now she couldn't figure out what had even compelled her to be so aggressive in the first place.

"Are you sure that you are truly converted?" asked Micah.

Malinda's face turned bright red. "Well, yes, I am pretty sure. At least, I think I am a Christian."

"How do you know?" asked Micah.

"I have gone to church all of my life," she replied. "Plus, my daddy is in charge of the Sunday school department."

"Going to church does not make you a Christian," Micah explained, "any more than being in an apple tree makes you an apple. The Bible says, 'By their fruit you will know them.' A true believer wants to serve, obey, and follow God with all of their heart. They hate the sin in their own heart more than they hate the devil. They want to be just like Jesus in their nature and character. I'll be honest with you, Malinda. I am not judging your heart, but I do not have a very strong inward witness that you are right with God. My heart should bear witness with yours that you are saved. If you die without giving Jesus all of your heart, you'll split hell wide open, but you don't have to. Jesus came to earth and paid the price for all of the sins of mankind. You can accept the free gift of salvation and become what the Word of God declares is 'a new creation.' But you are going to have to repent of your self-centered life, believe God raised Jesus from the dead, and give Jesus your whole heart. You're going to have to deny yourself, take up your cross, and follow Jesus wherever He wants to lead you."

While Micah was speaking, the conviction of the Holy Ghost fell upon Malinda. Tears began to run down her face, causing her make-up to smear. "What's happening to me?" she asked.

"That is the presence of the Holy Spirit upon you. He is calling you home to Him, Malinda. God deeply cares about you, and He has a purpose and a plan for your life. The devil wants to kill you and mess you up, but God wants to save, deliver, and heal you. Will you let Jesus have your heart and take complete control of your life, Malinda?"

"Oh, yes. Please, Micah, I'm tired of feeling empty and being someone I'm not. All of my life I have sat in this church feeling like I didn't belong, and now I know why." Her voice was filled with a tremble, brokenness, and sincerity as tears rolled down her face.

"Okay, then pray this prayer with me, and mean it with all that you are," said Micah.

As Malinda prayed for God to cleanse her of all of her sins and to give her a new heart, the presence of God's love flowed through her whole being, cleansing, washing, healing, and making her feel brand new. She glowed with newness of life.

"I feel so different, so clean inside," she said. "I have never felt this good before!" She wept almost uncontrollably with joy.

Micah took her into his arms and held her, as tears of joy also flowed down his cheeks. It was not a hug of physical desire but one like a brother holds a sister when something good has happened to her. In this case, it was a sister who had come to life from the dead.

Chapter 13
More Opportune Moment

Belee walked back and forth, moaning and muttering to himself. His ugliness was amplified tenfold by the concern etched upon his face.

"Now what am I going to do? Every time we set up this Micah's downfall, it blows up in our face. Him and his cursed devotion and love for God. If only he were lukewarm, then we wouldn't have all of this mess. Lukewarmness allows us to germinate like food going bad in a warm room. How can I keep Raw-ah and the powers that be from finding out? It's a good thing that even lucifer himself isn't omnipresent and all knowing."

Belee paused, deeply troubled by his thoughts. "Well, I can't do anything about it right now anyway. He is totally engulfed in the divine light of God's presence. Something is going on, and I don't have any way to find out. I'd give my third eye and my soul to find out. I just know that it's nothing but more trouble. That's all it is, just more trouble, and I already have enough of that right now. I may not get him at this moment, but I guarantee there will be another opportunity. When he is least expecting it, that's when we will be there."

Belee began pondering the future and looking back on the past. "Right now, the most important thing for us to do is damage control. Raw-ah is requiring me to give him a report. I know I can't lie. He's got thousands of snitches looking to advance themselves. It's becoming a red zone around here. At one time, my sector was nice and quiet and pretty profitable. This town was full of rape, AIDS, cancer, and killings. There was no lack of robberies, pain, death, and prostitutes. But something is happening. Three months ago no one would dare open their mouths about our enemy, and now it seems like a day doesn't go by that someone isn't being stripped from our ranks. The devil help us, it's spreading like some highly contagious disease, and it all started with this blasted Micah. I curse the day he was conceived," Belee growled.

Belee was in the habit of speaking his thoughts and plans out loud to himself, muttering like a lunatic. There was no one else he could confide in. "His day is coming. I'll get him yet," he declared. "He'll make a wrong move, and when he does, that will be the end of him."

Leb'abreck and Tabeal were speaking as they stood over Micah on watch. "It's amazing," Leb'abreck said to Tabeal, "that it is by and through those who love God on this earth and in heaven that we are being made to see the ultimate purposes of God."

"Yes," agreed Tabeal. "To think that God would become a man to purchase himself a bride. Of course, I am talking about the believers. Not one drop of the precious blood that Jesus shed will be wasted, for all those who will love God to the end will be saved."

"And to think," Leb'abreck said, "that God knew before the beginning of time who they would be that would love Him on to the end. You know, Tabeal, that it is not easy for a human to love God in this modern age. For a person to truly love God with their whole heart, soul, mind, strength and being, they must be singularly fixed upon this purpose, or they will never be able to obey God and follow him. This whole world is a test and trial of their love for God. Of course, Thank God we angels have already been sealed into everlasting righteousness. We proved our faithfulness and love for God when we fought with Micah against lucifer and his followers. But a believer will not be sealed into God's divine character of love until he dies fighting the good fight of faith and love for God."

"And what a fight it is," Tabeal agreed. "Even the master declared that there would come a time when it would be almost impossible for a person to be a true Christian. Thanks be unto the heavenly Father that with Him all things are possible."

"But what a glorious day that will be when all things are finally fulfilled and accomplished," Leb'abreck responded. "When the new Jerusalem comes down out of heaven as a bride adorned for her wedding day, what singing and shouting there will be throughout eternity. Creation and God and His people will finally become one, and nothing will ever separate them again. Never will sin, disease, poverty, pain, or sorrow ever be seen or heard of again. It will all seem as if it was nothing but a terrible nightmare. For those who have loved and obeyed Christ, it will be a dream come true. But woe to those who have refused to repent, and have rejected the salvation that was offered to them through the blood of Jesus. For they will be forever damned."

"You know, Leb'abreck," Tabeal said, "I really feel that the great and final day of the Lord is nearly upon us."

"I agree with you," Leb'abreck said. "And seeing that the time is so short, we must really be on our toes and do all that we can to protect those who shall be the heirs of salvation."

Leb'abreck and Tabeal gripped their swords tighter, lifted their shields a little higher, and scanned the spiritual horizon with eagle-like eyes as Micah was on his knees crying out to God.

Chapter 14
Swallowed Alive

Micah went home that afternoon rejoicing in the knowledge that Malinda had come to know and love Jesus. Totally unbeknownst to him was the fact that she had been manipulated by the devil to seduce him and to lead him into a relationship that would sidetrack him and cause him to become lukewarm in his Christian walk. In which case, if he had died in that condition, God would have had to vomit him out of his mouth. But it had backfired; instead of Micah being deceived, Malinda had been born again and baptized in the Holy Ghost. Micah's heart felt like it would burst for joy. A supernatural expectation seemed to be resting upon him. So strong was it upon him that it took everything within him not to shout.

It was approximately 1:05 p.m. when Micah arrived at his apartment. It was his normal routine on Sundays to eat a small meal and to go to the local shopping mall to pass out tracts. But today was different. A deep urgency came upon him to pray. He went into his small living room and fell to his knees. Groanings of the Spirit flowed from his heart to his mouth. Compassion for the Lord and His will totally overtook him. Agony for the lost took upon flesh and blood in the realm of his emotions and intellect.

As he prayed, the Holy Spirit filled his mouth with a very unusual and frightening request. "Dear Lord, I want to reach out and touch those who do not know you. I know in my head that they are eternally lost and damned, but I need to see it. I need to experience it. I need to feel the agonies of the damned. Oh, Father God, if I am to be consumed with a true heart of compassion, allow me to have a supernatural experience of hell. In order that I would have a greater and deeper compassion, a deeper love, a deeper understanding for the lost, I want to know the pains and sorrows, the torments, the fears, and the agonies of those in hell. I want to weep and to wail, to travail in my heart over the unconverted in order to reach them more effectively with a broken heart."

At that very moment a very frightening, overwhelming darkness suddenly came upon Micah. Time itself seemed to stop. To his utter shock and amazement, the earth and the ground underneath him began to shake and tremble. The floor of the room opened up and Micah fell into a hole. Down, down, and down into a deep, deep, deep, dark hole he fell. The opening that he was falling down through seemed to be like that of a well, approximately three feet wide. It was an endless tube, and it went on for miles and miles. Through the years he had experienced dreams, nightmares, and hallucinations from drugs and alcohol which he had taken. But none of them ever came anywhere near to what he was experiencing at this very moment. It was so real that he could feel, touch, smell, hear, and see everything. Fear, anxiety, and absolute horror filled Micah's whole being.

As he was falling down this deep, dark hole, a violent and overwhelming hot wind blew from the bottom of the shaft and hit him in the face. With the wind came a suffocating, nauseating stench that made it extremely difficult to breathe. Micah lost all track of time and did not know how long he had been falling, it seemed to have no end. It was bottomless, or was it? As he looked down he saw that he was falling feet first, and between his feet, he saw what was at first a very small and faint orange, reddish glow. It began extremely small, but as he continued to fall towards the light, it became brighter and wider.

Then before he knew it, Micah was out of the black tunnel and had entered into a gigantic, seemingly never-ending cavern. Still he continued to fall like a skydiver tens of thousands of feet above an ocean of liquefied, swirling lava and blazing fire. It was a burning, churning, bubbling, boiling lake of fire, like a pan of hot molasses. He could see that it was extremely violent. Fire and brimstone were exploding upon its surface everywhere, sending flames thousands of feet into the air. The flames darted here and there like a huge, blazing gasoline fire, to appear one moment, vanish, and then to appear somewhere else. At the same time, there were air-shattering explosions like volcanoes erupting across this vast surface of liquid lava. It was a living, swirling whirlpool that pulsated and radiated like hot charcoal in a furnace with molten steel, liquefied stone, and swirling gas. Fire danced across the top of its surface, like miniature tornadoes spinning violently out of control, until they ascended up into the black nothingness of the cavern Micah was falling in.

As he continued to descend toward the surface of this endless lake of boiling liquid fire and lava, Micah felt heat so intense that his very skin and flesh felt like it was melting and being burned off his hands, face, and body. Yet, as he looked at his skin and flesh, it was still there. At the same time, he could smell a sickening gas that was more suffocating than anything he had ever experienced. He coughed and gasped violently, trying to get a breath of air, but there was none to be had.

In the midst of this pain, Micah heard an eerie, humming sound, like a throbbing moan that never stopped. As he fell closer and closer to the surface of the fiery liquid, the humming moans increased in intensity. This ear piercing, overwhelming sound grew louder and louder until it became more distinct and clear. It contained ear piercing highs and incredible heartbreaking lows that he could not describe. He wondered what this sound could be, and at that very moment God opened his understanding to what was happening. The sound was not coming from equipment, machinery, or something from nature. It was coming from human beings who were screaming and wailing and groaning with intense pain, unbelievable agony, and unbearable torments. Micah's ears were filled with the terrible screams of damned souls. His whole body began to shake violently with rivers of absolute dismay and complete horror as the bitter lamentations of suffering humanity engulfed him.

It was at this very moment and second that Micah realized that God had heard his prayer and had, for some strange reason, answered his prayer quite literally. There was no turning back; there was no stopping what had begun. He was headed straight for hell.

Chapter 15
Journey to Hell

Micah thought about the people he had heard say that they didn't believe in hell. He remembered many so-called ministers of the gospel who had said there is no hell, or that the souls of men will not burn forever but will be burned up. He had heard some teach that the fires of purgatory will cleanse a human soul of all sin and wickedness. But as Micah was descending into the very center of this inferno, he realized that these are all lies propagated by the devil and his demons, the enemies of God. "Man is an immortal soul, which means that we are eternal. We can never enter into a state of nonexistence. The scriptures give us the truth," his pastor had said recently when Micah had asked about it.

"Some would have you to believe that when we die we enter into a state of sleep or go to a place called purgatory," his pastor had said. "Some would even declare that we come back as something, or somebody, else. These are all the wishes of those who are hoping they do not have to stand before their Maker. But they will have no choice in this matter. The Bible says that hell is a great, fierce and irresistible fire, a dark, unquenchable and everlasting fire! And sin, which is selfishness, is the gateway to hell. It is a broad and wide path which leads men to eternal damnation, separation from God, where there is never-ending anguish, unutterable sorrows, everlasting pain, and eternal torments." Micah now knew without a doubt that this was true.

As he closed his eyes, Micah could see his pastor earnestly pleading with the congregation. 'Sin is being self-centered, self-serving, and self-seeking," he said. "It is the vain pursuit of sinful pleasures. It is rebellion, mutiny, and disobedience to God and His Word, nature, and character. Hell is a prison for souls forever lost in their selfishness. It is a place of never-ending, searing pain of eternal damnation. Now you might ask if God is love, why would He create such a hideous place called hell and send man there? Because man is eternal, God had no choice but to create a place where rebels, sinners, and selfish people would be locked away forever. Please understand that God can not allow sin and selfishness into heaven. It would corrupt, pollute, and destroy all that God has created. Sin is the absolute opposite of all that God is. God is light; sin is darkness. God is selfless; sin is selfishness. God is pure good; sin is pure evil. Look at what sin has done to humanity! All of the wars, death, famines, disease, sickness, and crimes all the hate and strife, divorce, addictions, poverty, all hunger and pain is because of sin. Sin is selfishness that is locked up in the heart of a man. Sin is the DNA of the devil. Hell is the only conclusion of a life that is lived in selfishness. If there could have been any other way, God would have made it."

Micah could envision how passionate his pastor had been when he spoke on the subject of sin. "It is spitting in the very face of God. It is making yourself god, sitting upon the throne of your own heart. I beg you, with all the sincerity of my heart, to come out of your sins, turn from your wicked ways, change your mind, and give your heart, your soul, and your life to Jesus Christ. He gave Himself for you and you need to love Him with all that you are, with all that you have, and with all that you will ever be. If a man should gain the whole world and yet lose his own soul, what shall it profit him?"

Micah remembered how some in the congregation just passed off the sermon as foolishness. It was as if they didn't really believe that we would all someday die. But it does not matter who you are, or what you possess; we will all die, Micah thought. James 4:14 clearly states, "How do you know what your life will be like tomorrow? Your life is like the morning fog—it's here a little while, then it's gone." James 1:11 says that men are like the grass that dries up, or like the little flower which is beautiful for a brief period, but then it droops and falls.

Suddenly Micah was jerked out of his reverie. At about two thousand feet above the surface of the ocean of hell, the pain hitting his body was unbearable. As he looked down from his position, he saw upon the surface of the lake of fire what looked like little black objects that were violently bobbing up and down like fishing corks in the burning, churning ocean of hell. As his eyes focused, he could see thousands upon tens of thousands of these objects dotting the surface. They were everywhere he looked, and as he looked upon these objects, he found himself being possessed by an overwhelming curiosity. He lost interest in everything else that was happening. In spite of all of the pain that he was experiencing, his mind was very clear and sharp. A supernatural curiosity had gripped his mind and heart.

As he fell closer, he saw that these objects were actually oblong, not round, and they contained limbs at both ends. These limbs were waving back and forth in a frantic motion. A deep, tormented groan erupted from Micah's belly as he suddenly realized that these black bobbing objects were nothing less than human beings! Men and women, girls and boys, and teenagers were screaming, moaning, and yelling as they were being turned and tossed about, head over heels, carried along in the swirling lava of the churning undercurrents of hell. In his past Micah had heard people weeping and wailing over the death of a precious loved one. But never had he heard crying like this, such agony, such screaming sorrow and howls of pain. It tore his heart, for it was obvious that they were unable to control their directions.

These were souls forever damned, souls with no hope, no escape, and no relief from pain. Micah thought about the people that he had known who had died without loving Christ. Their hearts had been full of the lust of the world. Their lives had been full of selfishness and sin. They had no time for God or His word. They had spent their lives pursuing the pleasures of life, filling their minds with vain and useless amusements. The words of his pastor paraphrasing 2 Timothy 3:1-4 came to Micah's mind. *Understand this, that in the last days, it will be a time that will be very dangerous and difficult to be a Christian. For people will become totally self-centered. And because people are self-centered, they will love money. They will be lifted up with pride, and they will be quick to speak bitter words. They will have no respect for parents; they will be thankless, ungrateful, and wicked. They will not even care about their own families. Hard hearted, unforgiving, slanderers, they will be critical and fault finders. They will be without self-control, ugly and nasty in their attitudes with no love for what is right or good. They will even betray their own friends. Stubborn and bloated with self importance, they will love the useless pleasures and amusement of this world more than God.*

Micah's pastor had said that either we love God and forsake the world, or we love the world and will forsake God. We cannot love, follow, and obey both of them. These people who are in hell at this very moment, Micah realized, are ones God had called for so long, loud, and often, with such great fervency, just like He is calling people everywhere right now. And yet they closed their ears. They were stupid and senseless, blind and deaf to the warnings of God. Death chased them even as it does those living right now. The wrath of God hung over their heads just like it does unbelievers right now. Yet they cared not; they feared not. None of these things seemed to move them. It did not trouble their hearts that they did not love God or obey Him. They ate and drank, they bought and sold, they planted and built, and they went to work and came home. They even went to church, but they went on sinning and living as if they would never die. They were ignorant and senseless of their danger even as many are right now. They thought that God was nothing but mercy and forgiveness. No matter how sinful they lived their lives, they thought that the blood of Jesus would forgive them of sins that they refused to come out of. They did not realize that God hates sin and that He is a holy, jealous, and righteous God. Because He is a righteous God, He must judge sin. When they discovered this truth it was too late, for they awoke in this dreadful lake of brimstone, sulfur and fire, with no way of escape. There was no relief from pain, no hope for the future, and nothing to look forward to except endless torment. Their bodies burned black like chicken scorched on a barbecue pit. They are souls blackened by the unquenchable flames of a never-ending hell.

Caught up in the stark reality of what was going on before him, Micah did not realize that he was still falling, closer and closer to the surface of the boiling lake. Suddenly, he plunged into the lava, immediately sucking him in, swallowing him up in its hideous stomach of endless suffering. It covered him over and filled his mouth, nose, ears and eyes with an intense searing agony. The flaming sulfur of hell went down his throat, into his stomach, and filled his lungs. It was as though he was immersed in a baptism of absolute horror. His eyes felt like they were being consumed out of their sockets, and yet they were still there. His whole body was aflame like a wick on the end of a candle.

"This experience brought me to the stark realization that in no way could hell ever be exaggerated," Micah would later tell his pastor. "Everything I had ever heard or read about the eternal destiny of the lost, those who do not love God, does not sufficiently describe what I was experiencing. No words exist to describe the intense pain, the heart wrenching sorrow, the absolute agony, and the everlasting torments of hell."

Micah thought about how God warns us about hell. Why? Because He does not want us to go there. God has done everything He can to save, redeem, change, and convert us. He longs to help us. 1 Timothy 2:4 says that God "wants everyone to be saved and to understand the truth." 2 Peter 3:9 says, 'The Lord isn't really being slow about his promise, as some people think. No, he is being patient for your sake. He does not want anyone to be destroyed, but wants everyone to repent." God is so desperate to save us from ourselves that He gave His only begotten son to die for us, so that we could have victory over our sinful, self-centered lives. Romans 5:8 says, "God showed his great love for us by sending Christ to die for us while we were still sinners."

What awesome, amazing, mind-boggling, love! Micah realized. *Jesus Christ—Emmanuel, God in the flesh—took upon Himself the sins of the world, even mine.* The Creator, Author, and Maker of all things died upon the cross, so that we could be free from sin and selfishness. Sin is the gateway to hell; it is the broad and wide way that leads to destruction. Jesus is the only escape we have from our sinful natures, from the wrath and anger, tribulation and anguish of the righteous judgment of a holy God, in which we deserve to be damned.

Just then excruciating pain overtook Micah. It penetrated his mind and inflamed every fiber of his being. The lava was like burning mud that sucked him into the very depths of hell itself. Deeper, deeper, and deeper he sank. How deep he sank he did not know. The depths of the oceans of this present world are nothing in comparison with the depths of hell. It is called the bottomless pit, and Micah could not resist its current. It pulled and sucked at him like quicksand. Soon he had given up all hope of ever coming to the surface. He was covered and engulfed in total darkness and could not see anything. The Bible declares there is no light in hell, no light of the sun, the moon, or the stars, or even a candle. As he had been falling towards the lake of hell he had seen flashing, brilliant, explosions of fire. He later realized that God had allowed this because He wanted Micah to see what was taking place in the underworld of the lost.

As he was sucked deeper into the lava, brimstone and sulfur, the burning mud of hell was in his mouth and he could not breathe. Micah felt his lungs collapsing. He was suffocating, and yet he did not die. His flesh was burning, but he did not die. His brain was being ripped apart from the pain and sensations in his body, and still he did not die. The flames of hell burned his eyes, tongue, hands, and his belly. From the crown of his head to the souls of his feet, Micah was in excruciating pain. The searing brimstone and sulfur of hell penetrated every fiber of his being, but it could not kill him.

As he was going through these terrible sensations, Micah felt an upward thrust pushing him toward the top of the lake of fire. A strong current dragged him along, and then he came to the surface. He bobbed up and down as he moved along, turning head over heels, rolling and tumbling with the swirling masses of those around him. By now, he imagined that all of his feelings would have been burned into nonexistence and that all of his five senses would have been seared into nothingness, but that was not the case. Every one of his five senses were very much alive. He could touch, taste, hear, smell, and see the torments of hell. "Now I can tell you by personal experience that the most extreme and bizarre torments a person could ever experience on earth are like a mosquito bite compared to the never-ending torments of hell," he would tell his pastor later.

As Micah was pulled along, he noticed that there were other creatures in this boiling molasses of pain. They looked like large, extremely ugly, terrifying worms. They would come to the surface, disappear, return to the surface in another spot, and then disappear again. It was as if they were searching and hungering for something. Or was it somebody? It sent chills up and down his spine, even though he was in excruciating flames. Unconsciously, he found himself trying to hide from the worms, but he could not run or hide. About twenty feet away from him, a number of these large, ugly worms took turns breaking the surface of the lava again and again. Soon he noticed that they were headed straight toward him.

In less than ten seconds they were upon him. Not only were they upon him, but they were digging their way into him! They dug their way into his already-hurting, burning flesh. They burrowed and pushed, wiggling their way into his body. He could feel them crawling inside of him. Absolute disgust and dismay filled his heart and mind as they explored every part of his body. They even pushed their way up his spine and into his head. They would either squirm out of his ears or push their way past his eyes, coming out of the sockets, only to enter back into Micah's body somewhere else. He couldn't stop them or get them out. They were driving him insane!

There seemed to be no end to this nightmare called hell. A second dragged into an hour, an hour felt like a year. It was an everlasting eternity, and it was just the beginning of forever. *There is no end to this place called hell*, Micah thought.

There is no escape, exit, or way out. Hell is eternal; it is forever. Some might believe otherwise. But Malachi 3:6 says, "I am the Lord, and I do not change." Hebrews 13:8 states, "Jesus Christ is the same yesterday, today, and forever." His word is eternal. Heaven and earth shall pass away, but His Word will never pass away. *If God is everlasting, and His Word and heaven are everlasting, then so are the wrath, the anger and the judgment of God, Micah reasoned.* Revelation 14:10 says, "And they will be tormented with fire and burning sulfur in the presence of the holy angels and the Lamb."

Another distressing thought that came to Micah was that in hell there is no relief. There is nowhere you can go in hell to get relief. The torment will never end! *What a terrible price to pay for momentary pleasures,* Micah thought. *Why would anyone give up heaven? Yet people give up walking with God and eternity with Jesus for a life of selfishness in this world. These here in hell right now would go through anything, suffer any pains to get out of hell. But it is too late for them.*

As he was contemplating these things, another even greater torment began to flood his soul. It was emotional, spiritual, psychological, and mental. It was the realization that here in this slime pit called hell there is no love. It is totally void of love. *Even when I was a sinner*, Micah thought, *I was surrounded by the love of God. The goodness of God, the provisions of God, and the blessings of God are available to all as long as they are living on earth. People may not recognize it, but whether they know it or not, God is watching over them. I know He was protecting, helping, and reaching out to me, even though I was not serving or loving Him. A guardian angel was there all the time, though I could not see him.* Micah thought of the words of Jesus in Matthew 18:10, "Be careful that you do not treat one of these little ones wrong, for I am telling you, that in heaven their angels have uninterrupted access to My Father in heaven."

A loneliness and emptiness beyond description began to envelop Micah. Even though he bumped into many others like himself, there was no communication. There was no recognition of friends and relatives. Those in hell are tormented devils and souls, he realized. They are filled with dreadful screams caused by the fierceness of their pains. They shout fearful blasphemies against God's power and justice, which keeps them there. The torments of fellow sufferers do nothing to relieve these souls of their miseries. It only increases them.

On top of the physical pain and the agonizing loneliness, a thirst gripped Micah. It was a thirst so intense and maddening that he thought he would lose his mind. *If only I could have just one drop of water, just enough to wet my lips*, Micah thought. But there was none to be had. Hell is a lake that burns with fire and brimstone, but not one drop of water. There is no water in hell. Micah considered this. *Water is an illustration or symbolism of God's goodness*, he thought. *It represents His kindness, love, mercy, long-suffering, and patience.* Over eighty percent of Earth is made up of water in the form of oceans, lakes, seas, rivers, and ponds. At any moment we can drink deep of water, we can bathe in it, swim in it, and even drown in it. But once we are dead, once we have left this world in our sin, it is too late. Salvation is available now. But when we die it is too late. Throughout eternity one will be screaming and crying, begging and pleading for water. A person will be tormented forever with natural and sinful, unfulfilled desires. One's natural and spiritual, selfish thirst will never be fulfilled, never satisfied.

They will never be quenched; they will never end. As Micah considered the terrifying state he was in, he contemplated what he had taken for granted on Earth. Birds, animals, and all of creation display the unfathomable love of God. The shining sun, the green grass, the budding flowers, the blue gray waters of the sea, the light blue skies, the glowing moon, and the sparkling stars at night all declare God's awesome love for His creation. The beautiful fragrances that float upon the wind and the singing birds with their beautiful songs all reveal the goodness of God. God has blessed us and revealed himself to us by His awesome creation. God gave us the breath we are breathing, the clothes we are wearing, the food we are eating, and the body we are living in. It all comes from God. All that we have that is good and beautiful, lovely and beneficial comes from God. It is God's divine marriage proposal. Micah saw that God is calling, pleading, and asking people to follow Him into light everlasting. Jesus paid the ultimate price for the hand of His bride. He bought us with every drop of blood in His body. And He wants us to follow Him down the wedding aisle to the throne of His Father, to be one with Him forever. Micah realized what God is striving to do is to lead people to turn their backs upon their selfish lives. He is trying to get them to believe on the Lord Jesus Christ, and to walk in His divine nature of love so that they can be one with Him forever.

How long he had been in hell, Micah did not know. He had been crying out in pain and agony unconsciously, screaming like the rest of the damned. And yet his cries were of a totally different nature. Their cries were cursing, profanity, wickedness, begging and promises of repentance if given another chance. But Micah's cries were to God, justifying, praising, acknowledging that from God came his help, that God is righteous in His judgments, and that He is true and faithful and worthy of all glory and honor. Then from somewhere within, he cried out for deliverance. Even as Jonah prayed, he cried out to the Lord in his pain and suffering, and God heard him. In the midst of his prayer, a voice that seemed to come from heaven spoke. A majestic thunderous voice shook the very foundations of the lake of fire itself. And God said, "Let my servant go." The bowels of Hell twisted and turned as if it was in torment. It had no choice but to obey the voice of the Lord of heaven, earth, and hell. It spewed Micah out, and the next thing he knew, he was standing on the edge of a great chasm.

Chapter 16
The Broad-and-Wide Way

No longer was Micah floating in the fire and brimstone, but he was looking into it. Micah stood on the lip of a shear-jagged cliff that fell vertically, at least three hundred feet, straight down. As he looked off to his right, he saw a long, dark flowing river that was pouring its contents over the edge of the cliff and into the fiery mouth of hell. But there was something strange about this river, even eerie.

Not really wanting to, but somehow knowing that he must, Micah walked along the edge of the cliff toward the river. As his feet took him within a clearer sight of the river, Micah's heart pounded in his chest. He gasped for air and had difficulty breathing. He could barely believe what he saw before his eyes. The river was not flowing with water as he supposed, but it was made up of humanity—multitudes and multitudes. It was made up of all nations, tongues, and people.

As Micah drew nearer, he saw that they were walking on what appeared to be a wide asphalt road that wound its way as far as his eyes could see into the horizon. When the road met the edge of the cliff, it broke off with jagged edges that hung over emptiness as if a mighty earthquake created a huge sinkhole that ripped the road in half.

Micah studied the faces of those who were walking on this broad road. Most of them appeared not to be the least bit concerned at all about where they were headed. Many were laughing and jesting, some were simply engrossed in conversation, and others were caught up in their own problems. But not one of them seemed to be concerned about where they were going. They were headed for certain destruction with no comprehension or concern.

A totally different story began to unfold as the multitudes came within twenty feet of the end of the road. At that moment, the reality of their situation finally dawned upon their faces. As they were pushed forward, they would try to push back against the oncoming masses. But it was too late; they could not detach themselves from the onslaught of people. They were pushed forward, inch-by-inch and foot-by-foot. Those on the very edge of the cliff were struck with absolute terror and seemed to lose their minds. They pushed back with all of their might. They clawed, hit, scratched, and tried to crawl over the top of those who were unwillingly pushing them to their damnation. Screams of unbelievable horror came from their lips as they tried to hang on. As they fell over the jagged edge of the broad-and-wide asphalt road, they dug their fingernails into its unyielding granite-like surface. Unable to hold on, they continued to claw at the rough cliff walls, losing their fingernails and fingers and leaving trails of precious human blood behind. The cliff wall was covered and matted with blood, flesh, and bones.

As their bodies were engulfed in the flames of hell, Micah watched them for a few seconds as they struggled and fought while their clothes caught fire and their hair was consumed. Then the ravenous currents swallowed them up. They were male and female, young and old, rich and poor. They were the educated and illiterate, influential and unknown. They were people of all nations and positions in life. Hell does not discriminate, for unless a man or woman is born again, there is no escape from hell. Hell is no respecter of people. If this in itself was not horrible enough, then even more heart wrenching was the fact that this river of humanity that Micah was viewing was seemingly never ending. It did not slow up. It just kept coming unrelentingly, as far as his eyes could see. Micah's heart filled with unbelievable grief. Tears cascaded down his face like a waterfall. He began to cry out to those who were on the broad and wide road. He did all that he could do to try to warn them all of their certain destruction. But the majority would not listen. Many of them looked at him as if he had lost his mind. Others totally ignored him and looked the other way. A large percentage of them simply cussed and swore at him. He finally came to the place where he was not able to bear with their lack of response and concern any longer. He also could not bear what he was seeing as they fell over the edge of the cliff. So he ran away from the edge of the cliff along the road of the damned. He wanted to escape from the sight of the pain and agony that was etched upon the faces of the people as they fell into the abyss. He ran until he could run no more.

Finally, he slowed down to a walk. He saw something different in the distance. Micah could not make out exactly what it was, but whatever it was, it shimmered a brilliant white. It was not located on the broad-and-wide road, but it was directly off to the side of it.

As he moved farther up the road, he saw that the brilliant white object was taking on what appeared to be a cluster. As he looked out over the plain, Micah noticed that there were other clusters. Not just one or two, but many were scattered across the horizon. Some clusters appeared to be very large, but other clusters were very small, and still others were many in between. As Micah drew closer to the one nearest him, he discerned some type of movement within the cluster. As he got within a couple hundred feet of one of the clusters, it became quite apparent to him what it was.

There were people all grouped together in a circle, facing inward. Their backs were to the river of humanity (those who were walking on the broad-and-wide road) and to everywhere else. The closer Micah moved toward the cluster, the more the details became clearer. Those within these clusters had their hands lifted up toward heaven. Their smiling faces radiated immense joy, while other faces were marked with tears. At times one or more would break out in a prophetic word about how much God loved them and about the blessings that would overtake them in their walk with the Lord. Then it dawned upon Micah that these clusters of people in white must be Christians. These were believers who had been washed in the blood of the Lamb and were now wearing robes of righteousness.

The majority of these groups were almost identical. They were totally oblivious to the masses of humanity that were just a few feet away from them and going to hell. Enraptured in their own little spiritual experiences, they were singing songs of praise and worship. There was no denying their sincerity; it was evident in their involvement and the enthusiasm in their voices as they sang. *But what good is sincerity, blessings, and joyful spiritual experiences if you are not concerned about anyone else except your own little group*, Micah thought. *It's like sounding brass and tinkling cymbals.*

Urgency rose up in the heart of Micah. He tried to push his way into one of the clusters. As he did so, he found himself yelling and pointing to the river of humanity. It was not anger or disgust that moved him, not even self-righteousness, but God's love that was in his heart for the lost and damned. When he finally got their attention, they looked at him as one would look upon a lunatic.

"Look," said Micah. He pointed toward the broad-and-wide road. "Thousands and thousands of men, women, girls, and boys are only a short distance from your church, and they are headed right for hell. We have to do something. It is God's will that none should perish," declared Micah.

No one in the group moved. It was like they were in a stupor. Finally, one of the men spoke up. "Excuse me, brother, but God has not given us a spirit of condemnation, and to be honest with you that is not our ministry. Our ministry is to praise and worship God. We are to rest in His finished work on Calvary. You must not have the revelation that we are already complete in Jesus. God has met all of our needs according to His riches in glory in Christ Jesus."

For a moment, Micah was dumbfounded. Surely this man knew the context of these Scriptures, that all that Christ had accomplished for us was in order to equip us to reach the masses of those who do not know the truth. The only thing Micah could think of doing was to quote the Bible in its proper setting and to implore them to help him rescue humanity from the flames of hell, to fulfill the Great Commission. "God declared that their blood will be on our hands if we do not warn them," Micah urged. "We are to love our neighbor just as much as ourselves. If we do not love or care for their souls, who will?" But no matter what Scriptures he quoted, or what he said, they would not listen and he could not get them to move.

Micah stood there frustrated. He wept and cried uncontrollably, not only for the damned, but also for those who called themselves believers, those called to be ambassadors and witnesses for Christ. Somehow the enemy of their souls had deceived them into a place of spiritual pacifism. They thought they were spiritual, but in reality, they were self-centered and out of the will of God. God's heart was and is in the harvest field, not just in the worshiping, praying, and reading of His Word. The Scriptures clearly reveal that those who do not care for the lost are lost themselves. Micah fell to his knees under the burden that was upon his heart. The burden was not only for those on the broad-and-wide road, but also for those who called themselves "Christians." He closed his eyes and fervently prayed, "Father God, open the eyes of humanity and the church. Please forgive me for my lack of concern, commitment, and love. I pray that You, Father, the Lord of Harvest, will raise up laborers for the harvest field."

Micah did not know how long he prayed, but when he finally opened up his eyes, he was back in his apartment. It was after 9:00 p.m. and over eight hours had come and gone. From that moment forth, a greater burden than he had ever experienced before came upon him. He became desperate to reach souls for Christ.

While in prayer one night, just a day after his journey to hell, Micah became extremely desperate to reach the multitudes. A strange idea began to formulate in his mind. He was not sure if it was inspired of the Holy Spirit or not, only the Lord knows. Micah got up from his knees, put on his black leather jacket and headed downtown. He had made up his mind that no matter what it took, he was going to reach people for Jesus, even if he had to die doing it.

Chapter 17
Heavenly Warriors

Angels ascended and descended from heaven and earth. Excitement was in the air! Everything was humming as Leb'abreck and his troop prepared to do battle. What an awesome time this was. All of creation was in travail waiting for the manifestation of the sons of God. The consummation of great things was growing close. Yet before that final day arrives, many battles must be fought.

In the minds of most humans, angels float around in white clouds strumming harps and singing. But nothing could be further from the truth. Many of them are mighty warriors sent forth to do battle for those who shall be heirs of salvation. Angels are to bring strength to believers in the time of weakness and temptation. They watch, sober and protective, over their assignments. On this night, a clash was brewing once again between the angelic world and demonic entities over Micah's life.

Leb'abreck was consulting with Hodevah. Micah had declared war on the enemy and was going forth to set men free from sin and all of the devices of the enemy. He had no idea what would confront him or how close he was pushing the limits of God's grace. It's not that God is lacking in power or authority, but God cannot override His very character. For He is called the Father of Lights in whom there is no variableness, neither shadow of turning. "Micah does not realize that he, himself, has a lot to do with what the heavenly warriors can, or cannot, do," Leb'abreck said.

"Many of God's own children have been deceived into believing the lie that everything that happens must be the Father's will because He allowed or permitted it," Hodevah stated. "Yet Jesus clearly taught that God has given man the authority to bind and to loose so that the gates of hell cannot prevail against the believer who speaks, knows, and lives the truth. If Christians will simply pray in faith and speak the Word in the name of Jesus in total submission and agreement with God's will, believing what they say will come to pass, God's angels and the Holy Spirit are able to go to work on their behalf. But because they do not use their authority, or believe the truth, they are destroyed by the adversary."

"Yes, and it is extremely heart wrenching for us angelic warriors to stand back and watch God's sons and daughters suffer while evil spirits laugh at and mock them and God in the process," Leb'abreck agreed. "So many times they open the door for the devil and his demonic host by allowing continued and willful sin in their lives. Or they are ignorant of the promises given to them by the Lord to overcome the enemy."

"Unfortunately, angels are not allowed to step in where they have not been given authority or permission," Hodevah said. "Two thousand years ago, two legions of angels stood ready and waiting for the Master to call upon them, but Jesus never did. If Jesus would have called upon the angels to deliver Him from the cross, humanity could never have been saved. They stood in complete shock as they watched the bulls of Bas Han tear into Him with their mouths, as ravening and roaring lions. The assembly of the wicked enclosed about Him. They pierced His hands and feet and then crucified Him. He gave up the ghost, for this was God's plan."

Leb'abreck responded, "Tonight angels are hoping it will be different. It would be a glorious night of victory if Micah moved in faith and did not become presumptuous. In this day and age of self-gratification and unbelief, far too many of God's chosen are leaning more and more upon the ability of their intellect and their own natural and extremely limited talents. Instead, they should simply believe what God has declared by His holy men of old as recorded in the Scriptures."

"And yet there is a remnant who dare to trust and believe God more than the philosophers of the doubting masses," Hodevah pointed out. "It appears that Micah is one of the remnant that believes that God meant what He said and said what He meant. In the heat of the battle what a man is made of becomes apparent. For it is not what comes to you that makes or breaks you, but that which comes to the surface, out of the abundance of your heart. And even as one brave martyr for Christ declared before his death, 'a man is no fool who gives what he cannot keep, to gain what he cannot lose.'"[1]

---

1. This quote was found as a journal entry by Jim Elliot, who was martyred by the Waodani Indians in Ecuador in 1956.

Chapter 18
Enemy Territory

The pitch black caverns of the deep were filled with echoes of spine-chilling screams, eerie crying, ear-piercing laughter, and hysterical giggles. The air was quite putrid, like an enclosed pig barn with no circulation. There was absolute chaos and insanity. Such is the world of demonic spirits.

If you were able to see them with the natural human eyes, it would cause you to become sick to the point of vomiting. Grotesque creatures they are, ugly beyond any earthly description. And yet there are those who, through deception and illusionary images, can cause themselves to appear as angels of heavenly light. Such is their deception that the very elect are almost deceived. But the amazing truth is that their wretchedness is not yet complete. For their ugliness grows day by day. It is like a disease that once it has started it does not know any boundaries or limits.

These grotesque creatures were not always this way. At one time they were awesome, lovely, and beautiful creatures—creations of splendor and majesty. They had been the servants of the Most High, giving enthusiastically, harkening to the voice of their Creator. Those were the days of great joy when the sons of God sang together the glories of the kingdom. The Father shared with them every good, perfect, and desirable thing. Life was rich and full.

But that was many thousands of years ago before the great celestial war. It all began when lucifer, the son of the morning, raised up a rebellion against the Most High, who is the Author of Life, the Creator of all existing things. One-third of the angelic host pledged their allegiance to lucifer. They refused to see the obvious, that God is a holy and righteous God. He is not to be trifled with or to be disobeyed, He is a consuming fire. Those of the pre-Adamic race also chose to follow the great deceiver. At the command of lucifer, they went on a rampage against the heavenly host because they would not follow them.

The battle was long and costly. Micah led the armies of heaven. Surely one would think that one-third could not prevail against two-thirds. But such was not the case, for those who rebelled against Him took upon themselves the character of the devil, whom they followed, resorting to lies, false promises, manipulations, and deceptions. There was no mercy or honor in their actions.

When it looked like evil might prevail against good, Jesus stepped into the battle. Lucifer, with all of his combined forces, could not stand against Him. He and his forces were cast out of heaven down to earth until the last and inevitable day. Thousands of years have come and gone, but there is not a repenting bone in their bodies. Sin, the ultimate weapon they have used against God, has backfired. And now it is destroying them from the inside out, causing them to become more repulsive and ugly by the day. Their strength is not as it was in the days of glory.

"We have him now," croaked one of those in the gathering. "He has entered one of our strongholds. He has overstepped the boundary and gone too far. This overzealous fanatic will not survive the night. We will finally be rid of him and his constant interference." Shouts and laughter of hysterical glee broke forth as the demons planned their last and final conflict with Micah. Doom hung in the atmosphere like thick pea soup. The demons hovered in the air over Micah's head. Their sizes varied. Some were as large and husky as gorillas, while others were the size of spider monkeys. Each had his own particular area of expertise, from the physical realm of sickness and disease to the emotional realm of fear, pride, lust, and hate. There were those who could actually control the weather and natural circumstances. As one looked over their ranks, one could see that they were a battle-hardened group. Not one of them had less than ten scars, where angelic swords, spears, or arrows had broken their hides.

Chronicles of Micah

Arar (meaning, "curser"), an ugly, one-eyed, small impish demon, spoke up, "What about those angelic warriors surrounding him? They look extremely determined to keep us away from him."

Around about Micah stood all seven of his elite guardian angels. Their broad, flat fighting swords were drawn, and their eyes were fastened upon the demonic hoard hovering about forty feet away. Leb'abreck stood in charge of his troop. He was not a large angel compared to some of those in his troop, but size can be deceiving. Years of constant battles had hardened his spiritual muscles and caused his speed to be as quick as a lightning bolt. For over nineteen years, Leb'abreck had been the only one protecting Micah. He had fought with every fiber of his being to keep him alive. At times, the greenish putrid blood of the adversary had covered him from head to toe. He was not successful in every battle to keep the enemy from inflicting Micah, because Micah also weakened Leb'abreck's strength by his ungodly decisions.

Gil-bore and Saw-on stood beside Micah with their legs spread wide and their eyes fastened upon the black hoard above and around about them. The swords they held burned like flames of fire with a fierce blue glow. Gil-bore noticed a motion off to his right. It was a huge black image coming at him from out of the dark. Immediately, Gil-bore's reflexes took over. He swung his sword with a powerful sweep. As he did, his sword came into contact with a large battle-ax. As the flaming sword of Eden came into contact with this ax, made in the fires of the netherworld, it trembled for a fleeting second, and then it sliced clean through the ax head. Gil-bore continued the swing with a fluid motion. The blade found its mark upon the shoulder of this giant imp. The moment it hit this demon's shoulder, smoke and green putrid blood flowed forth.

A devilish scream of pure pain filled the air. The demon retreated, leaving behind his ax, his arm barely attached to his severed shoulder. Instead of the demon hoard retreating, they moved in closer like a pack of wolves who have just tasted blood, like sharks circling a sinking raft full of bleeding people.

Gil-bore looked over to his partner, Saw-on. With a gleam of battle in his eyes, he spoke with a calm boldness. "It looks like we are going to have a real battle on our hands this time, Saw-on."

"It sure does, it sure does," replied Saw-on. "And by God's strength, we will defeat them."

"Get ready, here they come," Leb'breck's voice sounded as the echo of weapons clashing filled the air and mingled with the screams and shouts of battle.

Chapter 19
Souls in the Balance

Micah walked through the street, his face set for serious business. Like an addict seeking a drug dealer when craving a fix, or like an alcoholic seeking a bar when desiring one more drink, Micah was searching. But Micah was not looking for such value-deficient and meaningless deceptions. No, those days were forever vanquished, because he had filled those areas of his life with One who surpasses all earthly pleasure. Jesus had come into his life, and all things were made new. He was indeed seeking something, though. It was the pearl of great price; it was for souls found wanting in the balance, those who were still held captive by the devil and his damnable lies. Micah's heart ached for the lost, now that he had just experienced what hell was like by a supernatural visitation.

As he walked, he prayed quietly under his breath. "Oh God, please give me fruit tonight. Lead me to those who have not heard, who do not know your mercy and goodness, and who have not tasted the expectation of eternal life. Devil, I speak to you in the name of Jesus of Nazareth. You will not in any way, form, or fashion hinder me tonight or cause me harm. I take authority over every demonic spirit, and I bind it. Angels of the Almighty, I release you in the name of Jesus to protect me tonight. You who are ministers to the heirs of salvation put a hedge around me as I go forth to do my Father's bidding. In Jesus name I pray. Amen."

Just then, as he walked past a very dark alleyway, he noticed a group of rather rough-looking characters that were all standing in a circle. Immediately he had a desire to go share the gospel with them. Without even considering the possible danger of confronting these men, Micah walked down into the garbage-littered alley. Rats scurried away into the dark recesses.

Without making a bit of noise, he walked right up to the circle of young men Micah's age. They had been left hanging in the balance with no solid direction for their lives. This area was in a total state of decay.

For some reason, they did not notice his presence. Without thinking, Micah stepped right into the circle. It was then that Micah noticed that they were passing around a joint. Each one took his turn smoking the marijuana, taking a deep drag, holding that breath for awhile, and then passing it on to the next recipient. Micah counted eight of them in all, not including himself, and finally the joint came to Micah. He took the reefer between his fingers and just held onto it.

After about two minutes someone spoke up. "Hey, man, who's hogging the reefer?"

"Like, what's going on?" spoke up another one. The eight young men looked to one another, wondering.

Micah took the reefer and held it a little above his head. "Hey, you guys, listen." As Micah spoke, all of the eight young men looked right at him. "This stuff can give you a buzz and make you high for a little while, but it's not the real thing. Now, if you take what I have, you'll experience a greater high, a joy that is unspeakable and full of glory, and you won't ever have to come down off of it either."

"Hey, man, who do you think you are, and where'd you come from?" A rough-looking young man by the name of Tony spoke up.

Micah just continued speaking, and for the next ten minutes he declared with holy zeal and love what God had done for him. "God is reaching out to all of you right now. Jesus cares about you, and He proved it by giving His life on Calvary over two thousand years ago so that you could be free from the bondage of sin and have eternal life and fellowship with Him. Jesus Christ is God's unconditional love to all who will come to Him with a repenting heart."

Amazingly, not one of them spoke a word or interfered with his preaching. The Spirit of God was moving upon them in a powerful way. A number of them were trembling and even crying. The fear of God was evident upon their faces.

"If you want to know this Jesus that I have been talking about…if you want to come out of your sins and give your heart and life to Jesus

Christ, all you have to do is step into the middle of this circle, and I'll introduce you to God and His Son. Your life will be forever changed."

Four of the eight simultaneously, and yet hesitantly, stepped forward. The other four stood there with their heads hanging down. It was quite evident that they were fighting an internal battle in order not to comply with the offer. Those who stepped forward prayed out loud with Micah to make Jesus the Lord of their lives. They prayed to follow, obey and surrender themselves totally to God's will.

"Whoa man, what's happened to me?" spoke up a big guy with a three-inch scar on his face. His name was Leroy.

"Like, man, I feel so clean on the inside. I've never felt this good before."

"Yea, I know what you mean," said Jake, who was one of the four who had stepped forward.

"That's the Spirit of God," replied Micah "When you gave Jesus your hearts, the same Spirit that raised Jesus from the dead came into your spirit and recreated you. You may look the same on the outside, but on the inside you're a brand new creation. You are no longer a sinner, but you are a child of the living God. You used to be a slave to your flesh, the world, and the devil. But now if you truly mean all that you prayed, you belong to God. And if you would die tonight, you would go straight to heaven." They drank deeply of everything he was saying.

The other four who had not responded just stood there. Their faces revealed they did not at all like what was going on, but they seemed to be frozen in place. It was as if some invisible force was keeping them subdued.

Micah took the names of the four young men who had accepted the Lord. He hugged his new brothers in the Lord, prayed with them one more time, and spoke for a while to those who had rejected the offer of repentance and salvation. He encouraged them not to run from God because no man knew the day or the hour in which he would die. And then Micah went off down the road looking for other opportunities.

After Micah left, one of the guys who had refused to accept the Lord, pulled a gun out of his coat pocket. It was a short-barrel .357

magnum. His friends looked at him with concern. "Hey, Tony, what are ya doing with the gun?"

"I had it aimed right at his gut the whole time he was preaching." Tony declared. "Why would you do that?" said Jake.

"Hey man, the guy could have been a narc or something, and I was gonna blow a hole in him the size of a baseball. It wouldn't be the first time that I shot someone for getting in my way."

"What stopped ya, man?" spoke up one of the young men who had refused to yield to the Holy Ghost and the Gospel.

"I couldn't, man. I had my finger on the trigger and was pulling it with all of my strength, but it wouldn't fire." Tony replied with a puzzled look on his face.

"Let me see it, man," spoke up the same one. "Maybe it's jammed." He took the gun, aimed it into the air, and pulled the trigger. A loud crack echoed off the building walls as fire and smoke flashed from the end of the barrel of the gun.

Micah was walking on a sidewalk heading into the heart of the town when he heard a gunshot go off behind him. He turned around and looked, but he did not notice anything unusual so he continued down the street, praying and hoping that no one had been shot by the gun.

Chapter 20
Gates of Hell

A sector of the spiritual world shook with unrestrained fear. Demons could not stand on their feet. A groaning and grinding sound surrounded them. It was almost like a natural earthquake in the sense that everything that could be shaken was shaking.

"What...what is happening?" vibrated the voice of Kakia (which means, 'haughtiness'), an ugly little imp whose face looked like a distorted toad.

A large demon by the name of Gaw-al (meaning, "castaway, loathsome"), who was on a higher level of authority, answered back with a deep tremble in his voice, "It is the beginning of a spiritual awakening in our sector."

"Hell forbid," screamed Kakia. "Can't we stop it?"

"That's just it," responded the grotesque large demon. "We have been doing everything we can with everything we have and still this little Christianite by the name of Micah keeps coming at us. The fire of the Almighty burns in his eyes. He is hungry for souls. Once that happens there is almost no stopping them."

As he spoke, the very foundation they were standing on shook. In the midst of their conversation, the whole demon population of that sector exploded in loud screams and curses. Another soul had just been rescued from their wicked clutches.

After all of the noise died down a little bit, the large demon, Gaw-al, continued his conversation. By this time other imps had gathered around. This was not just another demon speaking; he was one of their champions of deception, a master of disguises by trade. "Even as there is order and rank in heaven and on earth, there is also a semblance of complete stop. Even the angelic armies had to withdraw. After ten years, you could not even discern that there had been a spiritual awakening."

"Well, what was it?" spoke up Ma-har (rash), a spirit of impatience.

"Hold your tongue, I am getting to it. Really, it is quite stupid when you think about it. What was lacking in these Christianite's lives was the Word of the Almighty. They were sailing high on the feelings that come with a move of God. But when the feelings began to dissolve, they never moved into faith, which, of course you know, comes by the Word of God and confidence in what Jesus said. If they would have had the Word coming from their hearts and out of their mouths, there would have been no way we could have prevailed. If they had truly continued to love God, we could never have stopped them or have taken them captive."

At that moment, another tremor hit their sector. Some of the ugly host fell on their backs with the shaking. After the quake passed, Gawal continued. "What has really got us worried about this quaking is that this Micah and the church he goes to are building their whole experience on the Word. And if Holy Ghost conviction that has been built and established on the Word explodes, then nothing we can do will be able to stop it."

"Rumor has it that just a little while ago some of the fiercest warriors were overcome, and by only seven angelic soldiers. But what made them stand and prevail over two hundred of our experienced squads?" asked Ma-har.

"It was the mortal," answered Gaw-al. "He spoke and prayed that blasted Word, which in turn empowered them. If he had been ignorant to the truth, we would have had him lying dead on the street with his guts splattered on the sidewalk. But one of those angels put his finger behind the trigger of the gun to where our slave could not shoot it. Then another angel wrapped his arms around those four who stood faithful to our side and would not permit them to interfere or move."

As Gaw-al spoke, demons began to enter into the cavern, floating down through the roof. They came in limping, bleeding, and ripped up as if they had been through a threshing machine. They obviously had been in a battle and had received the worst end of the fight.

Gaw-al called out to one large, distorted demon. He was bleeding profusely where his shoulder and arm had been severed. "Hey Stugo (to hate), what is happening up there?"

"It's a demon's worst nightmare," croaked Stugo. "It's all falling apart. There is a maniac Christianite on the loose."

As Stugo was talking, an alarm began to blow throughout their quarter. "Battle stations, battle stations, we are under attack," came the squeaking voice of a demon on watch.

At that very moment, heavenly angelic beings began to sweep down out of the ceiling of the cavern. Their swords were drawn for battle. Screams of pain filled the air as imps and demons were put hard to protect themselves against the invading force. The gates of hell could not stand against this invasion.

Chapter 21
Revival Fire

If you could have been Micah's shadow, you would have heard him praying as he walked. "Father, thank You for those four new brothers. Strengthen them in their inner man. Open the eyes of their understanding. Help them to see, and know, and experience the truth. Father, I know that I have not even scratched the surface. There are so many who are lost and going to hell. They have never heard the truth; they have never had the opportunity to meet You in a personal way. Lord Jesus, please help me. I know it's Your will that all men would repent and renounce their sins, and that they would love You with all of their hearts. I know it's not Your fault. You long to move upon the hearts of all men and women. The harvest is so great, but the laborers are so few. Lord of the harvest, I pray that You raise up laborers." Tears flowed down Micah's face as he expressed his heart to the Lord. "Lord, I hunger to share You with others." An intense feeling of agony came upon Micah that some would call the burden of the Lord, and he wept with great sobs of agony.

As Micah cried out to the Lord, a question came to his mind. "Where is there a large group of people tonight? Where can I reach the most people in the shortest period of time?" As he prayed, an image of a large building began to formulate in his mind. The building became clearer and clearer; it was the local movie theater.

Micah knew that this new theater was always packed with people. If he hurried, he could make it before the next showing. He ran down the street, block after block, oblivious to the curious stares of bystanders. All he knew was that he had to get to the theater before the next showing. When he finally arrived, it was about ten minutes before the movie started. He pulled his identification SmartCard out of his pocket and purchased a ticket without even knowing what was playing. Not looking to the right or to the left, Micah charged past the popcorn and snack counter, past the soda fountain, and past the "coming attractions" information racks.

He entered the semi-dark theater and immediately noticed that it was full. "Lord Jesus, please help me find a chair." He walked down the aisle, row after row. As far as he could tell, every chair was full. When he finally reached the front of the auditorium, he noticed one empty chair at the beginning of the aisle. The rest were full. "Thank you, Lord," Micah whispered as he sat down.

As he sat there with his heart in his throat, trembling and waiting for just the right moment, Micah prayed quietly under his breath. "I wonder if I am doing the right thing," he thought to himself. *Oh, Lord, I do not want to bring a reproach upon the gospel, but Lord, at the same time, I cannot just sit back and watch them go to hell. I have to tell them the truth. They have a God-given need to hear the truth at least once.* Back and forth it went, an invisible battle between his mind and his heart. Micah looked at his digital watch and knew his time was running out.

Finally, right before the movie was about to begin, he stood to his feet and climbed onto the ledge where the bottom of the large panel screen connected to the stage. He stood there frozen for a minute, his heart in his throat.

"Hey, you. Get down from there!" someone screamed.

"Yea, what are you? You some kind of idiot?" bellowed another voice.

The whole theater erupted as people yelled and shouted curses at Micah.

Micah opened his mouth, not knowing where to begin or exactly what to say. "I am here tonight to tell you the greatest love story ever told." As Micah spoke, the holy presence of the Lord swept him away into the Spirit. Words flowed from his mouth like a mighty river, like a trumpet sending forth the word of love and warning to a lost and dying generation. A hush fell over the whole theater. Micah wept as he shared God's compassion for the human race. He preached that Christ came to the earth, was crucified on the cross for our sins, and resurrected from the grave for our redemption. But if any would reject this message, the only other recourse for God would be his terrifying judgment and anger.

Dr. Michael H. Yeager

As he preached, Micah lost track of time until thirty minutes had come and gone. As he looked around, he could see that the audience was gripped in total silence.

"Hey lad, come on down from there," said an authoritative voice. Micah looked down to where the voice came from. To his horror, it was a policeman—not just one, but two of them.

"Yes, officer," Micah replied. He crawled down off the ledge and onto the floor. The policeman who had spoken to him grabbed his arms and jerked them behind his back while the other officer placed plastic, unbreakable cuffs on him. Then each one took him by an arm and escorted him out of the theater.

During this time, Micah was oblivious to the reactions of the people inside the theater. If he could have seen their faces, however, he would have seen tears running down their cheeks. The conviction of God had blanketed them. As he walked up the aisle, past row after row, he did not hear one word from the audience, not even the movement of a chair or the rattling of paper.

He entered the foyer where a small crowd had gathered, curious about what was taking place. The lights on top of the squad car were casting red and blue shadows through the windows of the foyer. Micah noticed that it was beginning to rain outside, and people were opening up their umbrellas. One of the policemen walked over to a short, middle-aged man, who was slightly overweight and had gray hair. After a brief conversation with this man, he turned away from him and came back toward Micah. "Well, son, we are going to have to take you in. You have caused quite a disturbance here, and the manager needs to speak to the owner to see if he wants to press charges against you."

As Micah was escorted to the squad car, a newspaperman wearing a raincoat stood by the curb. He started snapping digital pictures and questioning Micah. "Hey, son, what ya do it for? Who do you follow? Are you with some new cult, or are you just high on crack?"

The policeman hesitated at the car door as if he were waiting for an answer. Without hesitation, Micah responded, "I did it because I don't want anyone to go to hell. The only one I am following is the Son of God, Jesus of Nazareth. And no, I am not on any kind of drugs."

Chronicles of Micah

The policeman then shoved Micah into the squad car, and they pulled away from the curb leaving the small crowd and the newspaper journalist standing behind in the rain. The older officer picked up a microphone and radioed into the main headquarters. "This is car 139 reporting in. We have picked up the suspect at the movie theater and are bringing him in."

"Roger, ten-four," a woman's voice responded over the radio.

This was not the first time Micah had been arrested. There had been a number of times in the past when Micah had been caught breaking the law. But this was the first time it was connected to preaching the gospel. No one spoke as they drove to the police station. The silence was unsettling. Unknown to Micah, however, was the fact that these two officers were at the theater during most of his outburst. They were in the vicinity when the call had come in about a disturbance in the theater. As a result of the message they heard, the Spirit of God was weighing heavy upon them. An intense battle raged in the mind and the heart of the older policeman. All of his life he had pushed off the notion that there was a God. Even the government early in the new millenium had concluded that the belief in God or in a so-called Savior was detrimental to world peace and the New World Order. They declared that Christians were an enemy of enlightened thought and definitely not politically correct. Those of the older generation who believed this were not tolerated, and since euthanasia had become an accepted practice, these people were disposed of, slowly and quietly of course, to avoid a public outcry.

However, when the older policeman had been a young man, someone had given him a Bible. He had read the whole New Testament. What he had read had been absolutely amazing to him. Healing and miracles seemed to be an everyday occurrence in the lives of those who believed in Jesus. They also seemed to rise above the immorality and weaknesses that once had laid claim to their lives. He had never met anyone who was really consumed with the message of Jesus, let alone someone who even believed it, at least not until now. This young man was definitely convinced of what he had been preaching, and there was a zeal and a supernatural power about him.

The officer was not the only one touched. Back at the theater something extremely unusual was happening. After the policeman had led Micah away, the manager set about trying to get things back to normal. He had the technicians get everything ready to start the movie. He simply would have to hold off the next showing for at least half an hour. The movie started with the usual normality; however, not everything was the same. Behind the audio and the special effects, crying could be heard. At first, the sound was very slight like the rustling of dry leaves in the fall, and it came only from one section in the back. Then the volume grew and spread like fire on a dry pine tree. People began to weep and cry everywhere. Some even cried out in voices filled with remorse and sorrow, moans, and sobs.

Upstairs the main technician running the 3-D projector and control panel did not realize what was happening initially, but he could tell something was not right. Looking around the booth, he tried to figure out what was wrong. Then he heard a low, muffled sound, barely recognizable over the movie. He knew it was not the production because he had heard the movie at least a dozen times already in its previous showings. The sound seemed to be coming from below in the audience. The hair on his arms and the back of his neck stood on end. Something definitely was not normal. He had a strong sense of an invisible presence that to him seemed spooky.

Ever so slowly, he crept down the stairs from the projection room, his heart pounding in his chest. At the bottom of the steps, he cracked open the door. Not being able to see what was happening, he opened it the rest of the way and stepped out into the theater. A wave of glory hit him like an avalanche. Weeping, crying, and praying people were kneeling at their chairs. Some lay flat on their faces in the aisles; others were crumpled up holding their heads between their knees. As he looked at the people, the conviction of God grabbed hold of him also. Instantly, he saw and felt his own true spiritual condition of being lost, damned, and headed for hell. All of the good things he had done in his life that he was relying on to get him into heaven, if there was such a place, meant nothing. He had broken the laws of God; he had sinned. Up to this moment, he really had not even believed in the power of darkness.

Public education had taught him that there was no right or wrong. He had been trained to believe that whatever made one feel good was socially acceptable. Man was his own god, and no one had the right to suppress anther's constitutional freedom. The leaders of the day and age declared there were no moral absolutes. If you believed otherwise, you were not politically—or socially—correct.

But now this officer was faced with reality. He knew in his heart now that he had been lied to. He began to cry and then weep. Sobs shook his body. He fell to his knees, asking, begging, and pleading for God's mercy.

Down at the police station, the officers escorted Micah into the building. At the front desk, Sally, a young woman with long brown hair, said, "What's up, Sarge?" Then taking a glance at Micah, she asked, "Hey, is this the nut who was preaching in the East Plaza Theater?"

"Yeah, we just came from there. I thought you would have known we were coming, I radioed in and told June."

"Well, I haven't had a chance to talk to dispatch. Our phones have been ringing off the hook throughout the station. Desk personnel were busy answering the phone calls, writing notes, and asking questions."

"What's going on?" he asked.

"Well, believe it or not, Sarge, it has to do with that little fanatic of yours."

"What in the world are you talking about?"

"Something really weird is happening at the theater."

"How can that be?" the sarge wanted to know. "When we left there everything was back to normal. The movie was just about to begin."

"I don't know myself, Sarge. I couldn't make a lot of sense out of what the manager was saying. He said something about people crying all over the place, and it was spreading. Even his hired personnel were being affected. He hit the main emergency switch that turns off all of the special effects and projector, kicked on the lights, but it did not seem to help. It's the strangest thing I have ever heard. Then, people who were just walking past the theater started weeping and crying. Some are even on their knees out on the sidewalk. They're kneeling in the rain!"

"It just can't be," whispered the Sarge, a strange far-away look in his eyes.

"What can't be?" spoke the younger officer, who was his partner.

"It sounds just like what my grandma used to tell me about. I was really young, but I can still remember some of her stories."

For a while no one said a word. Their silence was a voice in itself. The American people had been promised so much through federally-mandated policies like the New World Order school systems and medical and health care provisions. Instead of being helpful and effective, it brought tyranny and inefficient, non-compassionate bureaucracy.

"Well, what were her stories?" the clerk asked in a whisper.

All this time as Micah listened, he felt the presence of God descending upon the station. He saw it moving in the hearts of these policemen.

"It sounds like what my Grandma used to call a revival. She said when the Spirit of God came, people would become so convicted of their sins that they would start to cry and then weep. It became so overpowering that all they could do was fall to their knees and repent. And that's not all," the officer continued. "It would spread, almost like it was contagious. Factories and whole communities would come under this invisible power. The only way things got back to normal was by having preachers come and preach to help get people right with the Lord, as she called it."

As he spoke, tears welled up in Sally's eyes. Trying to fight them off, she took out a tissue, turned her back towards the two men, blew her nose and wiped her eyes.

"Ah, come on, not you, too, Sally," said the young officer. "You can't believe this baloney. It's just silly religious babbling. What's happening over at the theater has nothing to do with God. It's probably some new type of natural disaster caused by the ozone being destroyed. Hey, Sarge, you don't believe that stuff your old religious grandma told you, do you?"

"Did I say that I believed it? All I'm telling you is what she told me happened in what she called revivals. The similarities of her stories and this just struck me as sounding very close to the same. What I have to do right now is figure out what has to be done with his kid. Did you speak to the chief about this yet?" he asked Sally.

"No," she said, dabbing at her eyes with the tissue and sniffling. "He is in one of his real bad moods again. He hasn't been the same ever since his wife decided to divorce him."

"I thought that was about completed," spoke up the young officer.

"I guess it is," she responded "He hasn't really been confiding in anyone. He just stays in his office all the time."

"Hey, Sarge, what do you want me to do with this kid?" The young officer the whole time had a hold of the handcuffs behind Micah's back, every now and then pulling up on them, causing pain to shoot through his shoulders.

"I don't know," said Sarge. "I would like to just let him go. But it sounds like he has started something down at that theater that is not going to be easily dealt with."

"Should I book him then, and lock him up?" asked the young officer.

"No, not just yet. I think the chief really needs to see him. Then he can make the decision," said the sergeant.

"Better let me buzz him first," spoke up Sally. "Hello, chief. Sergeant McDonald is here to see you with a prisoner."

"What are you bothering me for? I told you I was not to be disturbed for anything. Anyway, McDonald has been on this police force for over twenty years. He can handle whatever it is," growled a voice over the intercom.

"I told you he wasn't in a very good mood," whispered Sally.

Let me talk to him," replied Sergeant McDonald. The sergeant pushed the talk button on the intercom. "Chief, this is McDonald. I really think you need to see this lad. He has started something that there is no law for or against…unless we call in the politically-correct police."

McDonald knew that would stir the chief up. Most of the regular policeman despised the politically correct police. They were similar to the KGB or SSI. If you didn't see things as the New World Order did, you were down the river. Nobody in his right mind wanted the politically correct police around. It meant trouble for sure for everyone. They were like the Gestapo of Hitler's day.

After a long pause, the chief said in a tone of disgust, "Okay, Sergeant, you've got me, so this better be important. My desk is stacked full, and I have a lot of backed-up paperwork to get done. You better come in first and leave him out there. I want you to explain the situation to me."

The sergeant pushed past a set of small swinging doors located near the side of the front desk and knocked on a decorative dark oak door.

"Come on in," a voice responded. The sergeant disappeared through the door, closing it behind him.

Micah was left standing under the close scrutiny of the younger officer. His heart pounded and thoughts bombarded his mind. Was he truly in the will of God in what he had done? Was it the Holy Spirit that had motivated him or just his flesh? Were they going to lock him up? Did he bring a reproach upon the gospel? As he stood there many thoughts and questions flooded his mind. And yet, wasn't God moving back at the theater? Weren't people being convicted of their sins? Even if they locked him up, it would be worth it, he reasoned.

The sergeant stepped out of the chief's office. "Okay kid, the chief will see you now." The sergeant held the door open for Micah as he walked into the office. The chief sat in a leather chair behind a big oak desk.

The chief was a large man with steel-gray eyes. His hairline was receding, but he was not what you would call bald. His whole demeanor spoke of emotional hardship. The minute Micah saw him all fear and intimidation left him. It was not that the man could not produce that type of an effect. In fact, it was quite the opposite. There was no doubt that this was one tough hombre. But all of the fear and intimidation that Micah should have had was driven out by the love of God in his heart. Divine love, agape love, flowed through him for this police chief. He did not see him as a threat, but as a lost soul headed for hell. He saw him as a man whom the world had used up and was now about to flush down the commode of life.

"Take a seat," grunted the chief. "The sergeant told me what you did at the East Plaza Theater. What kind of scam you got running? Or have you become a religious nut? Before Micah could answer, the chief continued, "You see, son, I pulled up your records." The chief pulled out a computer printout and pushed it towards Micah. "According to our records you are no stranger to police stations. At thirteen you were arrested for destroying private property. At sixteen you were taken in for possession of alcohol, dope, and for driving under the influence. The list goes on. According to a special report in our computer, we were setting you up for a bust on selling illegal drugs. But it seems you got wind of it and went cold turkey. Now all of a sudden we find you in a theater preaching hellfire and damnation. What's going on with you? Your brain burned out or something? Have you been sniffing airplane glue?"

"No sir," replied Micah. "I'm not into drugs or alcohol anymore. I have found something, or I should say Someone, much better than all of that garbage. Let me tell you what happened." Micah shared his pains and hurts, his past mistakes and failures. He told how he stood in a dump of a motel, a cockroach-infested bathroom, ready to slit his wrist when the presence of God came and touched him. He explained how he had a total transformation of his life.

The police officer interrupted with a harsh voice. "Stop right there, son. Save your preaching for the low-life scum out on the streets. I'm not going to hell!"

"With all due respect, Chief, how do you know you're not going to hell?" asked Micah. "The Word of God declares that all have sinned and come short of the glory of God. There is none righteous, not one. According to 1 Corinthians 16:22, 'If anyone does not love the Lord, that person is cursed.' To love God is to obey God and His Commandments."

As Micah continued to speak, the chief sat wooden in his leather chair, engrossed in what Micah was saying. His mind was silently screaming to him that everything Micah was saying was only for those who are simpletons; only for fools who were living in a make-believe world, for the gullible. Yet his heart was ready to burst. Wave after wave of conviction was flooding his innermost being. His whole life seemed to flash before his eyes in slow motion and yet faster than the speed of thought. He saw his struggles, sins, mistakes, and his selfish ambitions. He saw the compromises he had to make to get where he was. *What good had it accomplished?* he wondered. His childhood sweetheart had become his wife, but she had left him. How could Maggie leave him?

112

And then she had been given custody of their three children. Everything he really loved had been stripped from him. There seemed to be no future, no reason to go on. What good was life when you have no one to share it with?

He had fought and clawed to reach what the world would call the pinnacle of success. And now that he had arrived, there was nothing there but loneliness and emptiness. Just one more step higher, one more advancement and then he would experience the fulfillment, the joy of what was to be the ultimate satisfaction of his life. At least, that is what he had told himself. But every time it was the same, just a shallow, momentary happiness that quickly vanished. His desire to be a police chief had driven him until it destroyed his family. He had found out too late that all of his life was empty vanity.

But maybe it wasn't too late. Maybe, just maybe, what this young man was saying is what he had been searching for his whole life. But what good was it anyway? You can't teach an old dog new tricks. And even if he could change, how could God ever forgive him after all of his lies and manipulations. What about all of the lowdown, underhanded things he had done? He had sold his soul to the New World Order for position and power, for the pleasures of this world.

As these thoughts raged in his mind, he heard Micah quoting Scripture. Something about Jesus came to seek and save the lost, that there is no sin or problem too big for God to deal with. All you have to do is believe, just believe. And then came a question the chief least expected. "Do you want to repent and renounce all of your sins? Are you ready to give your whole heart and soul to Jesus Christ?"

The moment the question was presented to him, a light flashed on the inside of him.

He saw a door of deliverance. It was a way to leave the old life with all of its ugliness. He had a revelation right then and there that his greatest enemy was himself. It might mean the end of his career, and life as he knew it, but so what. "How do I do that?" the chief asked.

"According to Romans 10:9, 'If you confess with your mouth that Jesus is Lord and believe in your heart that God raised him from the dead, you will be saved.' But you must recognize that there is nothing good in you at all. Jesus said you must deny yourself, take up your cross, and follow him wherever he might lead. You must open up all the doors of your life and give Jesus permission to come in to every area. Then he will make you a brand new person. Would you like to do that?" asked Micah.

The chief looked him straight in the face, for he had already decided. "Yes," he replied.

It was a very strange sight to behold, a big, tough police chief on his knees with tears flowing down his cheeks while he prayed his heart out to God. And kneeling beside him was a kind of wild-looking young man with one hand on the chief of police's shoulder and the other hand lifted toward heaven, his face also streaming with tears. They were tears of joy and happiness for what God was doing.

For a split second, there appeared to be translucent beings standing around them with their swords drawn, ready to bring judgment on anyone who would interfere with the prayers of these two mortals, these two humans who once were lost, but now were found.

Chapter 22
A Taste of Glory

Micah walked back and forth in his small front room. His apartment was more of an efficiency apartment than a full flat. His hands were lifted up toward heaven. He was rejoicing and praising God for all of the great things He had done. Never in his life had he ever imagined that Christianity was so awesome and powerful. He had heard about the miracles that Jesus had performed, but that was back when Jesus walked the earth in His human body. Now here he was, two thousand years later, experiencing the same experiences that the early church had tasted. Every day was becoming more exciting. The presence of God was upon him in ever-increasing measures; he was being filled to overflowing.

"If it gets any better, I don't know what I will do," Micah said to himself.

The presence of God was quite evident in that little apartment. As he continued to worship God, the presence of the Lord became much stronger. The love of God became so real that he could no longer stand up on his feet. He fell down on his knees, with tears freely flowing, until he was lying flat upon his face totally caught up in the presence of the Lord. And then, a pure bright and clear light appeared in front of him. A portal of light. In all its brilliance, Micah could barely look into it. He was petrified and did not know what to do. He was frozen on the floor of his apartment, unable to move a muscle. Fear gripped his whole body.

Out of this glorious light stepped the figure of a man, not an ordinary man. He was about six-foot, ten-inches tall with a broad chest and shoulders, but a slender waist. His flesh blazed like burning bronze. He had the stature of a body builder, but more solid and almost unearthly. He wore a white tunic, with a slightly transparent belt around his waist that glowed the color of gold.

Chronicles of Micah

"Fear not, Micah, servant of the Most High. For I have come from the presence of the Almighty to show you things that must come to pass."

To Micah it almost seemed like a dream. And yet he knew it was real. With trembling in his voice he asked, "What's your name?"

"My name is of no importance. I am but a messenger sent to you with a message and a mission that is greater than I."

Inwardly, Micah wondered what kind of purpose could there be in this encounter. In the back of his mind, a question floated to the surface. Dare he ask this supernatural being? He feared to do it, and yet he knew he must. "I must ask you a question."

"You may ask; it is for this purpose I have been sent," the angel replied.

"I am commanded of my Lord to try the spirits," Micah responded. "Who is Jesus of Nazareth?"

The angel responded with boldness, "He is my Lord, the Christ. He came to this earth in the form of a man, born of a virgin. He was crucified, died, and arose again from the dead. And He now sits on the right hand of the Father." Deep emotion flowed from this heavenly being as he declared this acknowledgment of Jesus' lordship. "Now you must come with me, Micah, son of the Most High. For there are many things you must see." The angel stepped forward, took Micah by the hand, and lifted him to his feet.

Micah found himself being led by the angel into the ball of brilliant light. As he stepped into the light, it flooded his whole being. All filthiness of the flesh felt as if it just melted off of him. His mind became clearer and more comprehensive than he had ever thought possible. Time itself came to a standstill; it became eternity. How Micah knew this, he did not know. It was something he simply knew without a shadow of a doubt. Many truths flooded his innermost being as he stood in this light, things he could not possibly have any way of knowing.

He whispered to himself, "I once was blind, but now I see!"

The light was just as bright, but he could see clearly now. It no longer hurt his eyes. The portal of light was some kind of doorway into another world. Before him lay a very long corridor. The heavenly being disappeared, and not knowing what else to do, Micah walked down the long corridor by himself. Yet, he was not alone. He knew that his God was right there at his side, not in physical form, but in spiritual presence. He walked and walked and did not grow weary or tired. His mind and heart had never known such peace and tranquility. There were no fears, no cares, no sin, or sorrow. Just total harmony and serenity of spirit, soul, and body.

Suddenly, he was out of the light. He entered into a place so beautiful and incredible that it temporarily took his breath away. There, stretched out before him as far as his eyes could see, was a majestic and indescribable forest. The trees were gigantic in proportion. There were redwoods, taller and wider than the redwood forests in Oregon or California, reaching to the heavens above. Upon the hillsides and plains were beautiful flowers growing in perfect uniformity, as if a gardener with the most exquisite taste had planted every one of them. The emerald-green grass was the perfect length, not too low and not too high. As he gazed across the landscape, he saw animals large and small, too numerous to count. There were deer, rabbits, and a lion eating grass. A small family of bears was splashing in an almost-transparent river that flowed down from a snow-white mountain range unlike any on earth.

The water tumbled its way down the mountainside, creating waterfalls here and there, until it once again found its way down the river seeking the lowest place of gravity. As the water fell from the side of the mountain, it created a half a dozen or so multi-colored rainbows that stood out as if they were three-dimensional.

Micah had no words to describe the beauty he saw. Instead he stood frozen in place, overcome with that which lay before him. Finally it occurred to him that his hearing had become extremely sensitive. His ears seemed to be able to pick up sounds that were miles away. Not only could he hear everything, but also he could distinguish it. He heard bees going from one flower to another collecting pollen. He heard a slight breeze blowing through the grass on the plains, and a cow and its calf chewing their cud. A lion in the distance roared, not with the ferociousness of a vicious meat eater, but of a lion who was relishing its existence in harmony with its other fellow creatures. He could even hear the rabbits skipping across the grass. He heard all of these distinct individual sounds, yet it was not annoying or confusing like the mad

117

rushing about that goes on in the cities of men. It was more like a beautiful orchestra being conducted by a divinely gifted maestro. Such a symphony has never been heard upon the earth.

At almost the same time, Micah noticed the vivid colors. They were of such deepness, clarity, and brilliance. All of the artistic geniuses of his day and age could never even create on paper, or even with the most high-tech graphics, anything as near to perfection as this was. Not only was there an almost supernatural clarity to his sight and hearing, but also to his sense of smell, taste, and touch. It all seemed to be magnified a hundredfold. If there had been a magnification of these scenes in the natural world, it would have revealed the blandness and ugliness of the world, because of the corruption of sin. But in this place of glorious beauty, it simply revealed the exquisiteness of it all.

The aromas that floated in the atmosphere filled his nostrils. The smells were very strong, but not at all nauseating, quite the opposite. To some degree, he could even taste through the sense of his smell. It was one of many delightful experiences that he was encountering in this heavenly place.

All of these things registered to Micah's mind and instantly he knew in his heart that he was in a part of heaven. In all of his imaginations of what heaven would be like, it never once entered into his mind that it would be like this. Revelation knowledge flowed through his soul as he realized God's original plan, that earth was to be a miniature version of God's divine habitation. But man's rebellion, his disobedience in yielding his will to satan, had opened the door, a Pandora's box of disaster, pestilence, disease, perversion, and corruption which turned the earth into a mockery of God's original plan. What was meant to be heaven on earth had become a hellish nightmare.

While pondering these thoughts, Micah noticed that he was standing upon a road that wound its way down into the gigantic redwood forest. Instinctively, his feet began to move him down the road, which was built with beautiful, multicolored stones. When he finally arrived, he realized that he had walked over five miles, but amazingly he felt just as relaxed as when he began.

He noticed also that there was no fear in the animals. There were quite a number of different species along the road and on the road, and none of them fled from him. It was as if all of creation was in harmony, and he was not a stranger, but an intricate part of this heavenly place. It would be so nice to walk down through the meadows, to sit by the bank of the beautiful river and let his feet soak up the crystal clear waters. He could just imagine the assortment of fish that were probably swimming therein. It would be so nice to stay right here forever. Yet there was an urgency in his heart. There was something that must transpire while he was here. He knew that it was somewhere at the end of the road he was standing on.

He stepped into the forest, under the towering canopy enfolding him with comfort and security. Light filtered down through the branches here and there causing shimmering reflections of light to shine off the leaves of other trees that were growing under the huge canopy. The ground, tree trunks, and large rocks and boulders were covered with many colors of moss, and the moss was exquisitely placed as if by professional design. Ferns, some large and many small, stretched through the forest in perfect arrangement.

The path led straight into the heart of the forest. There were no bends or turns as far as Micah's eyes could see, but it was as straight as an arrow flies. He walked down the path at an easy rate, taking in as much as he could. Once in a while, there was a stone bridge on the path, which took him over bubbling, sparkling, transparent water. At the stream Micah would stand on the bridge and look into the water, watching schools of fish swim by. They were bright and beautiful like coral reef fish back on the earth, but much more exquisite and beautiful.

As he continued to walk, his heart overflowed with love for the One who created all this. How far and how long Micah walked he could not guess, but it was long enough to expect that the sun would be going down. However, there was no change in the light. It was just as bright as when he had arrived.

Chapter 23
Divine Commission

As Micah continued to walk, everything was so peaceful. Majestic trees stood to the left and right of the seven-foot wide path and they were filled with birds such as cockatoos, canaries, doves, parakeets, and finches, to name just a few. The light filtering in between the trees glistened on the birds of such magnificent beauty and variety. There were large and small birds of colors and species beyond count. Their voices echoed throughout the forest, and Micah had no doubt that they were singing praises to God.

Micah was so caught up in the wonder and beauty of it all that he did not even notice that the angel, who had been with him at the start of his adventure, had returned.

"Do you see all of these splendid and beautiful birds, Micah?" the angel asked. Amazingly, Micah was not at all surprised by the return of the angel. In heaven there is no fear, sickness, or sin. There is nothing but joy and peace, tranquility beyond description.

Micah turned and spoke to the angel, no longer as a superior but a fellow companion in the plan and purpose of God. "Sir," Micah said, "Do you not think that these birds are the most beautiful things you have ever seen?"

"Do you understand what it is the Almighty is revealing to you?" the angel asked. At this Micah turned once again and looked at the angel. "What do you mean?"

"These birds you look upon are a shadow of those things which will come to be. For even as these birds are of many different species and colors, so in your future will you have an effect on many cultures, tongues, and nations."

Micah's mind seemed to go numb for a moment. It just did not seem to make sense. "I am awfully sorry, sir, but I don't have the foggiest idea what you mean," replied Micah.

"Servant of the Most High, be it known unto you that what you see is a shadow of the souls of men and women who will be brought into the kingdom because of your obedience and hunger for the Lord. Many will be set free from the bondage of sin. Multitudes of almost every nation, tongue, and tribe will hear the glorious truth, and that truth will set them free. They in turn will go forth in the power and presence of the Holy Spirit and will take the name of Jesus to other nations, even as you have done, and will do, and drive back the forces of the adversary. For the day of the Lord is at hand, and a new day is about to dawn. Strengthen your heart. Be strong in the Lord and the power of His might. Hold up the arms of your brethren; wash their feet, humble yourself, be a servant and the Lord will lift you up. Help those who are called and anointed but have none to assist them. Under-gird and encourage them to fulfill the call of God upon their lives."

The words of the angel penetrated Micah's heart. He fell to his knees crying uncontrollably. God had spoken to him. He would never be the same again. The Lord did have a divine purpose for his life. He was called of God, sent forth by the Almighty to set others free. It was not to be a one-man army; he was only one gear in the majestic machinery of God's divine purposes. But it was joy unspeakable and full of glory. How long Micah wept, he did not know. The next thing he realized was that the angel was gone, and he was no longer in the woods.

Chapter 24
Under Siege

Leb'abreck was virtually exhausted as he held his sword in one hand and his small round shield in the other. Six fellow angels with him were standing shoulder-to-shoulder in a circle with their backs toward the center, and Micah was lying in the middle of the ring. The Spirit of God was upon him. The angels did not know exactly what the Lord was doing in Micah's life, but the adversary had been trying to break through the ring of angelic warriors. They had received orders not to let anything happen to or disturb Micah. Whenever there is a visitation from God, it is a guarantee that the enemy will try to interfere.

Just then, ugly, monstrous shapes seemed to jump right out of the walls and ceiling. Red eyes burning with sheer wickedness peered from their distorted, hideous faces. They held barbarian-style weapons in their claw-like hands. They held clubs with long razor sharp spikes. They held swords that were round, half-moon type forms, bars with a chain and spiked ball at the end. Some had spears with razor-sharp ends. They looked like trolls and ogres of ancient fables—lizards that walked on two claw-like feet. They came as a horde, depending upon their sheer strength and numbers, to overrun the angels of God.

As they stormed toward Leb'abreck and his band, they appeared like hyenas attacking a small flock of sheep. Leb'abreck lifted his sword preparing for the first blow and at the same time called upon the Lord of battle for strength. Immediately, the strength of the Almighty flooded Leb'abreck's whole body from feet to hands.

With mighty swings and bold shouts, the angels fought against the demonic horde.

Green blood flowed as limbs were severed from bodies and heads rolled upon the floor. As the battle proceeded, the angels were pushed back toward Micah, but a source of divine strength flooded them, and they once again drove the aliens back.

The demons were self-centered cowards at heart. When they realized that they could not win, they scattered in seven different directions. Those in charge who were in the back of the horde screamed and threatened, but to no avail. Finally, the leaders also turned and fled. Behind them squirmed the severed limbs of the horde. The limbs that could, crawled after their owners.

The angels were all covered with the disgusting green blood of the enemy. They also had cuts and wounds, but they continued to worship God for the victory. The angels know that it is only by His strength that they are able to stand up against these vicious assaults from the enemy.

Leb'abreck readied himself for another attack, knowing that after the forces of hell had licked their wounds and recovered their composure, they would be back once again. One thing the powers of darkness do not have is quitting sense. But neither do those who are sent forth to minister to the heirs of salvation. It is an honor to serve the Lord in this great conflict, even though it brings much pain and affliction, not only to the human race but also to the heavenly realm. It is well worth it, however, because when everything is said and done, great blessings will be bestowed upon the valiant and obedient.

It was not too long before the opposition's marching feet could be heard. Leb'abreck braced himself for another attack, having total confidence that when the Lord is on one's side, he cannot be defeated. One may suffer afflictions and go through trials and tribulations, but out of them all, the Lord will deliver His righteous ones.

Chapter 25
Before the Throne

Micah found himself in an immense place. So large was this room that he could not see the ceilings or the walls. The floor was a sea of crystal, radiating and pulsating with ever-changing colors that flowed through it like an incoming wave of the ocean. In the distance, Micah saw lightning flashes moving from one point to the next. Not knowing what else to do, he moved toward the phenomenon. As he drew closer, Micah heard thunder that sounded like mighty trumpets. With every step his heart beat faster, for he was approaching what looked like a gigantic throne.

In front of the throne and around about it were the most awesome creatures Micah had ever imagined. There were four of them altogether, full of eyes in the front and behind. The first was like a lion, the second was like a calf, the third had the face of a man, and the fourth beast was like a flying eagle. They each had six wings and the inside of the wings were full of eyes. When he was yet a great way off, even before he saw them, Micah heard these beasts declaring with a loud voice, "Holy, holy, holy, Lord God Almighty, who was and who is and who is to come."

Even more majestic and splendid than the throne was the One who sat upon the throne. He appeared like the brightness of translucent jasper. It was a light of such intensity and holiness that had Micah not been in the Spirit realm, it would have slain him. At the right side stood the Son of Man, clothed with a robe down to His feet, and about His chest He had a breastplate of glistening gold like that of a Roman general. His hair radiated like white wool, more pure than the whitest snow. His eyes burned with divine love, like a flame of fire.

Micah knew without a shadow of doubt that he stood before God the Father and the Son, Jesus Christ. Around about them shone an emerald rainbow much clearer and more colorful than ever conceived. Micah fell before the throne, quivering and shaking before the presence of his Lord and God. Then a voice spoke, sounding like it was coming from everywhere. It filled his mind and heart with peace and strength. The voice was one of love, and yet one of absolute complete and total authority with holiness. It was the voice of Jesus.

"Hear what we have to say to you, Micah, for you are a chosen vessel," Jesus said. 'Before you were conceived in your mother's womb, I ordained you and called you to be a prophet of these last days. For time as man has known it is coming to an end. I have placed My Spirit and My anointing upon you. My word have you hid in your heart, and I know that you will go where I send you and do as I direct you. Fear not the faces of men, for they will be as chaff before the fire and as dust before the wind. That which I say unto you is for days and seasons yet to come. It has been sealed into your heart, and at the appointed time it will be brought back to your remembrance."

Jesus continued, "I also say unto you, beware for there are many false prophets. They have gone forth in my name to deceive, if possible, the very elect. Their message is a message of health, wealth and prosperity. They are like the false prophets of old who declared peace, even though I had determined punishment and destruction. I cannot continue to allow the willful sins of humanity. These false prophets speak a message that will not cause humanity to repent of their wicked ways, to turn from the flesh, and to be saved.

Micah lay on his face in the presence of the Lord, hearing unspeakable words that could not be uttered with the human vocabulary. His inner man was drinking deep the mysteries and divine plans of God. Secrets that are not lawful to be spoken from human lips were revealed to him. Tears flowed from his eyes and down his face as he listened to the Lord. The glory of God was upon him. He lay there whispering "Thank You, Jesus" over and over. He did not understand with his intellect what had transpired, but he knew in his heart that he had a divine mission to accomplish, and by God's grace, he must accomplish it. Then it was over. The Spirit of the Lord whisked him away from the throne of God.

Chronicles of Micah

The next place he found himself was on a sidewalk in what looked to be a low-income area of a city. Coming down the street toward him were two rough-looking men. As they caught up with him, Micah found himself sharing the love and good news of Jesus, as well as the reality of divine judgment if they would reject the sacrificial work of Christ. As he continued to speak about the reality of Christ and that there is no way to the Father but through Jesus, he noticed that their faces began to distort until they looked at him with faces filled with absolute hate. Their eyes glistened with a hideous satanic appearance as they turned into demons right before his eyes.

Before Micah could even raise his hands in self-defense, they began to hit him in the face and the chest. After numerous blows, Micah finally fell to his knees. As he did, they kicked and stomped down on him. In the midst of this persecution, no hatred or malice emanated from Micah's heart for his attackers. Instead he prayed out loud, "Father, forgive them, for they know not what they do." Then Micah blacked out.

When he came to, he found himself lying on the floor of his apartment. He looked around the room expecting to see the angel, but there was no one there. It was late in the afternoon. At least five hours had come and gone since the angel had appeared. Micah had no doubt that his experience was no dream. The reality of everything that had transpired was eternally embodied in his mind and heart. He could see it all just as clearly as if he were still there. Whether or not he had been in his body or out of his body, he did not know. God had a special divine mission—a job to do, a purpose to fulfill. No devil in hell, no temptation great or small was going to rob him of the reality of it. With all his might, he was determined to fulfill God's will for his life. He would not disappoint Him who had chosen Micah to be a soldier.

Chapter 26
The Trap is Laid

Darkness, an intense, impenetrable blackness filled the air. It was an evil, nauseating, sticky, perverted, sickening blackness. Out of this blackness came voices, not loud and boisterous, but whisperings like that of hissing snakes. Within the hissing and whisperings, plans were being made. In utmost secrecy, the demons plotted strategies of death and destruction.

"We have found a major weakness, your most wickedness. It is even as we had hoped it would be."

"Don't play games with me," hissed the wicked one. "Just tell me what it is."

"Lust, your wickedness. Lovely, disgusting, perverted lust. It is the same weakness we have used against men of renown. If mighty men of old could not control their flesh, then surely this 'greenhorn' of a Christianite will not be able to. We destroyed Samson and King David with it. And was it not that the weakness of Solomon, and many others?"

"Yes, yes," responded the ruling spirit, Gaw-al, with an angry hiss. "I know all of that. What do you think I am—an idiot! What I want to know is what has led you to believe that he is vulnerable in this area. You tried once before to destroy him with one of our tidbits, and what happened? Not only did you not succeed in deceiving him into sin, but also this revolting son of a Savior led her into the camp of our enemy. We lost her because of your assumptions. Not only her, but those who were close associates of hers through her own testimony."

With much hesitation, the voice of Kakia, a naughty and malicious spirit responded. "Well, your wickedness, it is not exactly blatant things he is doing that brought us to this conclusion. But, it is the seemingly insignificant things. It is the ever-so-slight turning of his head when female humans go by, the looking at catalogs and magazines."

"You mean he is into pornography?" asked the ruling spirit with glee in his voice. "No, not exactly."

"What do you mean 'not exactly'?" growled Gaw-al with an angry hiss.

"It's…it's when he comes across a sales catalog," answered the lesser demon, his voice dripping with fear, knowing the pain the ruling spirit would inflict upon him if he did not like what he heard. "He lingers in the women's lingerie section. When he goes into work places where the children of disobedience have pornography on the walls, his eyes constantly dart across them."

"Enough of your yakity-yak, Kakia. Tell me what your plan is!"

"Yes, your wickedness," Kakia squeaked. "Last time we were too bold, too outright in our approach. But this time, we will be very slow and meticulous. We will entice and lure him by very small degrees, entrapping him by his own weakness. It will be like hanging a man. The weight of his own sin will snap his scrawny neck."

Kakia continued, "We will use a lukewarm, love-hungry, self-centered lassie. Oh, she acts just like a disgusting believer all right, but she is one of those we adore: a church-going, flesh-pleasing, carnal one. She has learned the art of manipulation and deception to get what she wants. All of her life she and her parents have been churchgoers. Her parents saw the conniving of their daughter, but they laughed it off. She is a perfect weapon. With her we will be able to seduce this spiritual zealot. He won't even know what hit him until it is too late."

"When will this take place?" demanded Gaw-al.

"It has already begun. The intricate pieces of the puzzle are coming together even as we talk. Seducing imps are at this moment working on the victim. Before he can help himself we will have him involved with her to the point of no return. And once he crosses that line, his effectiveness will melt away like an ice cube on hot asphalt. And if she conceives his child in the midst of their fornication, then most likely he will end up marrying her. And because we know what he does not know, it will be the end of his so-called preaching."

'What is this so-called information you have?" whispered the leading spirit.

"The loving, gentle, so-called beautiful girl is actually a nagging, bickering, spoiled brat. When she was a little thing, we planted within her a hatred for the ministry, and she decided and declared right then and there that no husband of hers would ever preach or be in the ministry."

All quietness was shattered by loud grotesque laughter. "I like it, I like it," Gaw-al laughed hysterically. "It just might work, it just might work."

Chapter 27
Is It Love?

Micah was actively pursuing the Lord's will. Five weeks had come and gone since he had stood in the presence of God, and the reality of God's purpose in his life burned in his heart brighter than the morning sun. He longed with everything within to please Him that had given His all for Micah's salvation. Yet there was something pulling at his insides, a nagging sensation that everything was not as it should be. He had prayed and asked his heavenly Father what was wrong, but there did not appear to be a reply. Micah examined his life meticulously. Heaven forbid that he should miss the Lord's will. His heart ached to think that he might be doing something contrary to the Word of God or that he might do something in the future.

Unfortunately, Micah had not yet realized that spiritual battles were constantly taking place between good and evil. It was not a battle against flesh and blood, but against principalities and powers, against spiritual wickedness in high places and rulers of the darkness. He had not realized that the devil was as a roaring lion seeking whom he may devour. He did not know that he was to walk by faith and not by sight, or emotions. But he knew that something was most definitely wrong. The only thing different in his life was a young lady. But how could that be the problem? He wasn't really that serious about her.

Her name was Stacy, and she was a really sweet girl. She attended the same church Micah did. Her father was one of the elders of the church, a real solid brother from what Micah could see. Stacy was involved in a number of different activities in the church. She also sang in the choir. God really had blessed her with a beautiful voice.

As Micah thought about it for a minute, that wasn't all God had blessed her with. The other girls at the church easily could have envied her height, the proportion of her body, her beautiful complexion, her long blonde hair, and her large blue eyes. She was a real knockout and she was affecting him physically to a certain extent.

It was not like she was coming on to him sexually, but he was having to deal with wrong desires. Their relationship had not brought them into any physical contact, except he had kissed her lightly a number of times after a date. Come to think of it, he might have been coming on to her just a little too strong. What bothered him was that she did not seem to resist his advances in the least. It was really quite the contrary. All of her actions appeared to be saying, "Here I am, and I am all yours for the taking."

As Micah thought about his relationship with Stacy, the phone rang. He walked over to the kitchen counter to answer the phone. As he pushed the appropriate buttons and picked up the earphone, the video screen lit up and the smiling face of Stacy appeared. "Hello," said Micah.

"Hi, Micah," drawled the very sweet and tender voice of Stacy. "I am calling to see if you want to go swimming with me."

"I don't know, Stacy, I really would like to go, but I was going to spend this afternoon in prayer and study of the Scriptures."

"Oh, come on, Micah, don't be a party pooper. You need to get out and have some fun. I am sure the good Lord doesn't mind," cooed Stacy with a voice that would melt the bravest of hearts.

"Well, I really don't think I should."

"You're simply a darling, Micah," Stacy purred. "I'll be over in about ten minutes to pick you up." She started to hang up.

"Wait," Micah spoke up. "Where are we going swimming?"

"I was going to take you down to White Sands Beach. Have you ever been there?"

"No, I don't think so," replied Micah. "But you know, Stacy, I really do not want to be around a lot of people that are scantily dressed."

"Oh, you'll be okay. I know a lot of the people who go there and they are believers just like us."

It was about fifteen minutes later when Micah heard a car horn honking outside of his apartment. He grabbed a towel and a small paper bag and headed out the door. It was a beautiful Saturday afternoon. The sun was shining brightly, and the temperature was in the upper nineties.

Chronicles of Micah

Stacy was sitting behind the wheel of her red 1994 convertible Mustang. It was in excellent condition even though it was over twenty years old. Stacy was quite stunning with the sun glistening on her beautiful, long blonde hair. For a brief moment, Micah was at a loss for words when he saw what she was wearing. Her swimsuit was what some would have thought attractive, but to Micah it was a little bit too seductive and revealing. It was not a bikini, but Stacy was so proportioned that it was embarrassing, Micah felt that way because ever since he had given his heart to the Lord, his opinion of what people should reveal had changed dramatically. Micah had read that after the flood Noah had cursed his son Ham for looking upon his nakedness. But Micah did not want to seem legalistic, so without saying a word he got into the front passenger seat.

Stacy leaned over and kissed his cheek. Then she put the car in drive and sped away from the curb, heading for the beach. As they went down the main thoroughfare, Stacy noticed the brown paper bag. "What do you have in the bag?" Stacy asked Micah.

"I brought some gospel tracts with me," replied Micah. "I thought we might have an opportunity to share Jesus with someone."

Stacy became very quiet. She seemed to be a little upset about it. "Is something wrong?" asked Micah.

"Well, I guess not," she replied very slow and hesitantly.

"What do you mean, 'You guess not'?" He did not say it with any type of criticism, but questioning.

"Micah, I just don't know if the beach is the place for us to be pushing Jesus down someone's throat," she answered.

Micah was caught a little bit off guard. "Stacy, I'm not going to push Jesus down anyone's throat. But if the Spirit of God opens the door for me to speak to someone who possibly does not know the Lord, I'll be willing and ready to tell them about what God has done for me."

Stacy bit her bottom lip. For the rest of the trip neither one of them spoke a word. They finally came to the exit for White Sands Beach. Stacy pulled the convertible into the turn off lane. Slowing down she drove into the beach parking lot, pulled into a parking spot, and turned off the engine.

"Micah, I'm sorry. Will you please forgive me?" Stacy said. "I don't want to argue with you. I love you, and all I want is for you to be happy."

The last statement totally caught him off guard. "You what?" asked Micah.

"I love you," answered Stacy. At the same time she leaned over and kissed him passionately on the lips. She opened her car door and got out. "Come on, Micah, let's go for a swim."

She walked around the car past him. As she did she swung her hips in a very seductive manner. Micah did not resist the urge of watching her go toward the beach. He got out of the car, grabbed his towel and a large umbrella Stacy had brought, which was lying in the back seat. As he walked toward the beach he prayed a little prayer of desperation. "Oh, Lord, please help me." Back in the car sat the brown bag that Micah had left between the two bucket seats.

When Micah finally caught up to her, she had already spread a blanket out on the sand and was running into the oncoming ocean waves. Micah put down his towel and proceeded to set up the large umbrella over the blanket. He watched Stacy coming up out of the water, wringing the salt water out of her hair. *Man, she's gorgeous*, he thought to himself. When she reached their spot on the beach, she grabbed him by the hand and pulled him through the sand toward the ocean.

"Come on, Micah," she said laughing. "Stop being so serious. Let's enjoy our time together."

He followed her into the water, at the same time grabbing her waist in order to tickle and splash her. The afternoon went by very quickly as they swam and dived, tickled, pushed, and splashed each other. Even though it was a very hot day, the crowd wasn't too bad.

In many ways Micah was enjoying himself, yet in another way he wasn't comfortable being out there. He used to enjoy being on the beach, especially at night when they would have parties, but now there was a nagging feeling deep down in his heart. As he looked around he couldn't help but notice the skimpy swimming suits that most of the crowd was wearing. He felt himself shriveling up on the inside; shame flooded his whole being. At one time he would have relished seeing all of the good-looking women in next-to-nothing swimming suits, but he no longer enjoyed it. Everywhere he looked there was flesh.

As Micah stood in the water, he asked himself how in the world he ever got himself into this mess. Then he heard someone calling his name. He looked up and saw that it was Stacy. Micah walked across the sandy beach to where she was lying on the blanket face down.

"Micah, be a darling and rub some of this suntan lotion on my back." She reached her hand out to him with a plastic bottle of lotion. It was then that he noticed that she had undone her swimming top strap. All that was holding it on was the sand under the blanket. If she would happen to roll or get up, she would lose it. He hesitated, not knowing what to say or do. She looked up at him with a twinkle in her eyes. "What's wrong, Micah? You look like you're deep in thought."

"Well, I just don't know if I should."

"Oh, come on Micah, I won't bite you. Besides, I can't reach my back, and you don't want me to get sunburned, do you? Don't worry," she laughed, "I'm not going to seduce you."

"Well, okay," Micah answered with a tremble in his voice. He got down on his knees, took the suntan lotion from her hand and squeezed it on her back. He rubbed it over her back down to her spine. As he did, emotions flooded his body like waves of the ocean. His hands trembled against her flesh.

"Um, that feels so good," Stacy purred softly, but just loud enough for Micah to hear her. "Don't forget my legs and my ribs." Slowly, but surely, a web was being wound Around Micah, like a fly being prepared to be eaten by a spider. Micah's hands rubbed the lotion on her legs and ribs. As he applied the lotion to Stacy's back, his heart smote him. He felt like finding a hole, crawling into it, and dying. Micah spoke up. "I am really sorry, Stacy. I really don't think that I should be doing this."

"That's okay, Micah, don't feel bad. I was enjoying it, but maybe you're right. Maybe this is not the right place or the right time," Stacy replied. "We'll wait till later," she whispered with a glimmer in her eyes.

Red lights should have been exploding inside of Micah. But he had taken the bait and swallowed it hook, line, and sinker.

It was late afternoon when they finally arrived back at Micah's apartment. As he was about to get out of the car, Stacy leaned over, wrapped her arms around his neck and pushed her body up against his. He smelled deep of her suntan lotion. She placed her wet, moist lips on his and gave him a passionate kiss. His head went dizzy. It was like he was falling down, down, down into a deep, deep, dark, slimy, black hole.

The next thing he knew, he was standing by the curb watching her drive away. The last thing he remembered her saying was something about church tonight. Then he remembered that there was a special Saturday night revival service with a guest speaker.

Chapter 28
Demonic Hysteria

The demons rejoiced, shouted, and laughed in the ranks as word came back about their targeted Christianite. Success was in sight; the enemy had been deceived. The one who had caused so much commotion and brought so much shame was about to be hung up by his hamstrings. Surely, he could not escape now. He had taken a taste of the delicate and addictive, poisonous morsel. The demons of lust had succeeded in penetrating his mind and blinding his spiritual eyes.

"It's working, your wickedness. We have him exactly as we planned," spoke Belee to a dark shrouded figure of a grotesque being. The air was heavy with the putrid stench of a rotting corpse.

"It is about time. I've been way too patient and merciful to you and your bumbling horde. I want this job done. There are too many other fires already burning from this Micah. If you would have killed him as planned, this never would have happened," growled Gaw-al.

Belee shook under the voice of his superior. He knew that he had to watch every word that he spoke lest the ruling spirit became angry. If that happened, his hide wouldn't be worth a toad's wart. Unbelievable torment and pain would be afflicted on his personage. "Your wickedness, he has already tasted the bait of flesh. You might say he has been bit by the bug: a demon bug," laughed Belee with a nervous crackle. Gawal did not laugh or respond. Belee continued, "I myself remain at his side night and day. I would still be there but your summons."

"What about the angelic warriors? Are they not interfering?" the ruling spirit demanded.

"No sir, it seems that their hands have been tied by this fool, of course. I am speaking about Micah. He is yielding his mind and body to our enticements. We believe that the lust has been conceived, bringing forth sin. And, of course, we all know that sin brings forth death."

"Yes death. Ha, ha, ha," laughed Gaw-al. "Lovely, God-severing death." His voice echoed off the cavern walls. Demons and imps trembled with dread at the evil sound of his laughter.

As Leb'abreck and six of his cohorts stood off to the side of Micah, demons laughed in their faces and mocked as they whispered deceptions in Micah's ears. Sorrow filled the angels' hearts, seeing that their hands were tied. Leb'abreck was unable to intervene on Micah's behalf even though he was a blood-bought child of the King. He, unknowingly, had opened the door to the enemy by yielding his mind and his actions to the lies of the enemy. Angels have very limited authority on the earth without the cooperation of men.

When God created man and placed him in the garden, he gave to him the dominion of the earth. Adam did not have to allow the serpent to beguile his wife, but instead he just stood there and watched his wife being deceived by the devil who had entered into the snake. Some of the heavenly host had been present when it all took place, but just as they are helpless in this situation, so were they helpless in the garden at the time of the great treason when Adam yielded himself to satan. That one action by Adam damned multitudes of humans to hell and turned over the authority of planet earth to the adversary, thus opening up a Pandora's box of death. That is why Jesus had to take on the form of a man in order to operate in the divine authority granted to man. Because He was sinless, He was not under satan's domain.

Leb'abreck was grieved in his heart because he knew that unless Micah repented, he could do very little to protect him. The longer Micah remained in sin, the greater the possibility of his life and mission being terminated by the enemy. He was like an airplane stalled and in a tailspin. Unless he pulled it up, soon it would be the end of life Micah had come to know it. A free will is a terrible thing when you use it to go against God's will.

Chapter 29
Lamb to the Slaughter

Two months had come and gone. Micah's relationship with Stacy was beginning to become hot and heavy. The subject of marriage had already been brought up a number of times. Even those whom Micah knew and respected were encouraging their relationship. People kept telling Micah and Stacy that they made a perfect couple, and they kept asking them when the big day was going to be. In the process, Micah had settled down to a lukewarm, traditional believer's life. He warmed the pew on Sundays and became increasingly less involved with God's work.

Then one Sunday night after the service, a sister in the Lord came to Micah and Stacy as they were standing in the back of the sanctuary. She was considered by some to be a prophetess of the Lord, and she even promoted herself as such. However, the pastor never acknowledged her claim by word or by action. She walked up to the couple declaring that God had spoken to her about them.

Micah stood there not knowing what to say. He knew that God did speak to His people by the supernatural gifts of the Holy Ghost. He had been moved at times by a holy unction. But this time, Micah just stood there not knowing how to respond. When he did not reply, she took it as a sign of his submission to her position as a prophetess.

"Thus saith the Lord thy God," she began. "As I gave Eve to Adam to be a helpmate and a companion, so I have placed Stacy into your life. Fear not and be not confused for as surely as Abraham had Sarah, and Isaac had Rebecca, so I have called you two together. So be bold and confident. Take her to be your wife, for I have placed my blessings upon you. Delay not, and do not hesitate, for I am not pleased with sacrifice, but with obedience. In your obedience, you will be blessed beyond your wildest expectations." The prophetess broke out in tongues, shook a little bit, and concluded with, "Thus saith God."

Immediately Stacy started crying. She wrapped her arms around Micah and hugged him tightly. Brothers and sisters around them came up to them, hugging them and shaking their hands. They congratulated them with "Praise God" and "Thank you, Jesus" utterances.

Micah felt like he was in suspended animation. His heart hurt like it had been pulled inside out. Instead of the prophetic word bringing peace, joy, and calm assurance, it brought anxiety and confusion. The prophetess had said, "Thus saith the Lord," and he did not want to disobey God. And yet something just did not seem to click. Somewhere in the New Testament he had read that the sons of God were to be led by an inward witness, not like in the old where individuals could not hear for themselves.

As Micah pondered what had just transpired, Stacy hugged those who were standing nearby. What Micah did not see, however, was that when Stacy hugged the so-called prophetess, she whispered something in her ear. She was thanking her for her help in convincing Micah that their relationship was divinely ordained.

Micah drove Stacy home that night. As he pulled up to her house she invited him inside. "I guess I could come inside for a couple of minutes," he responded. He knew that he must talk to her about the uneasy feeling that he had inside. He knew that he really liked Stacy a lot. Not only did he like her, but he had committed sin in his heart with her. Shame caused his face to flush as he thought about it. In his mind was the nagging question of whether he really did love her, and was this the will of God for them or were these desires he had for her lust and not love.

They walked up the sidewalk together. Micah had been to Stacy's house many times for weekly "home group" meetings, and he always looked forward to them. But this time, while walking past the well-groomed shrubbery and blossoming flowers, he didn't feel that usual inner peace. Stacy had placed her right hand into his left hand and was squeezing it as they walked. Micah couldn't shake that uneasy feeling; he felt like he was walking into a death trap. When they arrived at the door, Stacy fetched the keys out of her purse. She unlocked the door, opened it, and reached around the corner to turn the lights on.

The house was a very beautiful, large English Tudor. The furnishings were exquisite. Stacy's parents were quite wealthy. Her daddy, as she called him, was an executive for a major fiber optic communications company. As they entered the house, it was quiet.

"Aren't your parents at home?" asked Micah, even though he had a nagging feeling that they weren't.

"No," Stacy replied, "they went to my mom's parent's home for the rest of the week. Grandpa has not been doing very well lately."

"But I saw them at church tonight," Micah responded, hoping to hear that they would be arriving soon.

"Oh, they were at church, but their suitcases were already packed and in the car. They left about two-thirds of the way through the service."

"If your parents are not here, I guess I really need to leave."

"Oh no, Micah, it's okay. I know mom and daddy won't mind." She reached around behind Micah and closed the door. As she did, she let her lips brush his. Hot flashes went through his body. His inner man screamed, "Run for it," but his feet would not move.

Stacy took Micah by the hand and led him into their plush living room. The lights were off, but the moonlight shone through the big bay window. She wrapped her arms around his neck and began to kiss him passionately. For a while he tried to resist her. But it was too late. He was like a lamb going to the slaughter. The next thing he knew, they were lying on the plush white carpet. His neck was in an invisible spiritual noose, and the trap door was about to swing open.

There seemed to be no way to stop the hot passions that were flowing in his blood stream, when right out of heaven itself the fear of God fell upon him, and a Scripture burned into his heart. "Now the works of the flesh are adultery, fornication," the words literally screamed at him, "and they which do such things shall not inherit the kingdom of God." Micah unconsciously pulled away from Stacy and started to get up.

Stacy reached out her arms and put them around Micah's neck. "What's wrong, Micah? It's okay, I'm yours for the taking."

"No, Stacy, I don't want to take advantage of you," he said.

"You're not," she replied. "God understands we're only human, and we love each other."

"But it's not right, Stacy."

"I want you, Micah. I need you."

She was so desirable lying there in the moonlight. Micah's body shook with lust. He was almost out of his mind with ungodly desires, and yet in his heart he knew that he was at a major crossroad in his life, and he had already gone too far. Before Stacy could stop Him, he got up, and headed for the door.

"Where are you going, Micah?" Stacy asked.

"I'm going home," he replied, his voice trembling.

"Micah, don't leave. It's okay. We are going to get married anyway, aren't we? It won't hurt anything. I love you," she said.

"Stacy, listen to me. The devil has set us up. Sex outside of marriage is against God's will. It is sin. The Bible says there is a way which seems right unto a man, but it leads to death."

For a few seconds Stacy remained quiet. She lay in the moonlight. "Don't you want me? Don't you love me, Micah?" she cried softly.

Micah looked down at her, desire once again flooding his body. "Yes," he said softly, "I want you. But you're not mine to take."

He turned away from her and ran out of the house. Micah reached his motorcycle, took his keys out of his pocket, and inserted the key into the ignition switch with shaking hands. Leaning over to the right side, he pulled the kick-start pedal of his Harley away from the frame. He put his foot on the pedal and at the same time pushed himself up, with his foot pushing down. On the first try the engine kicked over. Putting the Low Rider into gear, he pulled away from the curb.

As he drove down the road toward his apartment, tears began to trickle down his face, leaving little lines as the wind blew against his cheeks. His unzipped coat flapped in the wind and helped to cool him off.

"Oh Father, forgive me. I have failed you. I've tread upon the precious blood of Jesus. Oh God, I'm sorry, I'm so sorry," he cried out.

The sound of the motorcycle drowned out his voice. The deep pain of repentance flooded his being. He sobbed until he could barely see where he was going. He thought back to where he had been spiritually just a couple of months ago. He recalled the fire that once burned in his heart and realized that same fire was almost gone. How could he have wandered so far away from God and not recognized it?

When Micah finally arrived at home, he took a lukewarm shower, turned off his lights, and went to bed. Almost immediately he fell into a restless sleep. As he slept, he found himself in a dream. In this dream he was entering into a very large bedroom. In the center of this room was a massive bed with silk covers and a brass frame. Lying on the plush fluffy covers of this bed were two of the most beautiful and desirable women Micah had ever seen. One of these ladies had long-flowing blonde hair, and her eyes were a deep hypnotic blue that seemed to swallow him up. The other one had coal black hair that hung down to her chest. Her eyes were also coal black, and they reminded Micah of a wild black panther.

The women seemed to be immediately aware of Micah's presence and began to call him and beckon him, reaching their arms out toward him. Immediately Micah felt an invisible power grab hold of him. It literally began to drag him toward the bed. He fought it the best he could. He leaned backwards against it, until his feet were in front of his body and his back was leaning against the invisible power. With everything in him, he struggled to stay away from the bed. But it was of no avail.

Step by step he was dragged toward the two women upon the bed. They licked their lips like two hungry wolves about ready to fill their bellies with their kill. Inch by inch he was dragged across the bedroom floor. He could hear demons somewhere in the background laughing, mocking him. It was as if they were celebrating and relishing in his defeat.

As he was dragged closer and closer, their eyes demanded all of his attention. As he looked into their eyes, a shiver of absolute horror flowed down his spine. For their eyes were filled with such an evil as Micah had never known before or thought possible. He knew there was no love whatsoever in their desire for him. It was nothing but absolute lust, and not just for him, but anyone else that was gullible enough to yield to their enticements. He also knew in his heart that once they had devoured him, it would destroy everything that was decent and godly in his life. They would wipe their mouth, as the Bible says, and declare they had done no wrong.

He was only about two feet from them now; there was no escape. Both women reached out (that is, if they really were women) to take his hands and pull him to them. He knew that he was trapped, caught, devoured by his enemy. He knew that they would consume him with their lust. As they finally succeeded in grabbing his hands, a cry came flowing from Micah's heart, out of his mouth. "Oh Lord Jesus, help me!" His knees hit the side of the bed. It was too late, they began wrapping their arms and legs around him like an octopus, dragging him screaming and kicking into the pits of hell.

Just as Micah gave up all hope, he was transported above the bedroom. In his dream he was looking down upon the bed. He saw the two women with hands upon his body pulling him toward themselves. As far as he could see, there was no avenue of deliverance. There were not even any doors by which he could leave the room. As they began to wrap their arms around his body, Micah noticed some type of movement off to his left side.

As he looked over in that direction, two of the largest men Micah had ever seen walked right through the wall. In height, they were over seven feet tall. They glowed with an unearthly light. Both had on large, white tunics, and around their waists were belts of transparent gold. On their chests were breastplates of the same material. They both walked with a confidence and boldness that was beyond description. As Micah watched this scene unfold, the hair on his neck and his arms stood on end. They were headed straight for his body, which was in a struggle against the two spirits of lust.

The next thing Micah knew, there were ugly, grotesque demons coming out of the walls, floors, and ceiling. It was as if they were out of some ghost story. They flung themselves at the two angelic men, but they could not stop them. Both beings flung the imps and demons off of them as if they were nothing but bothersome little spider monkeys.

As the angels got to Micah, one on the left, and one on the right, they grabbed him by the arms and the shoulders, picking him up as if he was as light as a feather. They pulled Micah away from the bed, ripping him out of the hands of the two women.

All of this time, Micah was looking down upon the whole scene. And then like a bolt of lightning it came to him who they were: angels of God who had come to deliver him from the snare and enticements of the devil. The angels turned their backs upon the women. With Micah suspended between them, they carried him to the wall of the bedroom. When they reached the wall, Micah found himself no longer looking down upon what was taking place but rather between the two angels looking at the wall. Then to his utter surprise, the angels stepped right through the wall, taking him with them.

Micah found himself sitting up in his bed. His hands were lifted up in the air, praising and worshiping God. He was in the midst of thanking the Lord for His supernatural divine intervention. The Spirit of God was upon him. Micah rolled out of bed, fell to his knees, and began to pray. It did not matter that it was only three o'clock in the morning.

For the next two hours the Spirit of God brought clear understanding to him of how the adversary had set him up and how he had missed God by yielding his mind and emotions to the wrong spirits. He repented for missing God, for not knowing the Word like he should have, and for not keeping his priorities right. As he looked over the last number of months, it was quite apparent that there was little fruit. With a deep and sincere commitment, Micah recommitted his life to wholeheartedly serve the Lord. In spite of what he had done, Micah was determined now more than ever to do the will of God and to destroy the works of the devil.

Chapter 30
Assignment

Leb'abreck was overjoyed. He had just returned from the earth. Activity was apparent everywhere. Angelic beings of different classes and ranks were coming and going, assignments were being given and completed. Moment-by-moment stories of glorious and splendid acts of faith were being reported. These stories had victorious, heaven-changing implications.

Unfortunately, however, there were also tales of heart-wrenching, eternal defeats, of humans being devoured and consumed by the enemy. Many of God's beloved children have the strange and harmful notion that God is in charge of all things and that whatever happens must be God's divine will, no matter how tragic or ungodly. Their ignorance thereby opens the door for satan and his demonic horde to have a heyday. Because of the lack of truth on the believer's part, some Christians do not understand that within their hands has been placed the authority to bind and to loose the powers of darkness.

The greatest joy of an angel of God is to be assigned to a believer who has awakened to the reality of who they are in Jesus Christ. An angel loves to serve one who speaks the Word of God with authority, one whose heart is filled with the Word and faith and who is walking in the holiness of God. When such a person speaks the name of Jesus, demons tremble and sickness flees. Nature must even bow its knees and obey.

So many of God's redeemed never come to the truth of who they are in Christ and what they can accomplish by His grace until it is too late and their journey on earth is finished.

All angelic guardians see born-again humans for who they really are: new creations, heirs and joint heirs with Christ. Humans are kings and priests, ambassadors of God, temples of the Holy Ghost. They are a building not made with hands, soldiers in the army of the Lord. They are those who will rule and reign throughout eternity with God. It is even understood by the angelic realm that the day will come when humans are to judge them.

"It is amazing to think that those who had rebelled against the Almighty, those created lower than the angels of the Lord, will rule and reign forever," Lebàbreck said aloud as he contemplated the mysteries of Gods eternal plan. "Those who literally had been the offspring of satan have become transformed by the grace of God into God's own children. How mysterious and unfathomable is the mercy and compassion of God's plan, to whom belongs all glory, honor, and power, forever and ever."

Six of God's mighty battle angels, Tabeal, Tsaphah, Nay-fo, Saw-on, Gil-bore, and Sawkal all walked with Leb'abreck. They were on their way back to the celestial city, just having returned from an assignment upon the earth. Earth definitely was not a lovely place to visit. Sin had taken its toll over the last six thousand years. The earth at one time had been beautiful, almost an identical copy of heaven. But it had been reduced to a quagmire of filth and pollution. Not only had the souls of men been steeped in stink and rottenness, but nature had gone into a state of regression. It was now a cesspool of hate, selfishness, and greed. And yet in this mess, there were treasures of great price, diamonds in the rough.

The angels spoke excitedly about Micah. "I thought we had lost him for a while there," said Nay-fo.

"Surely the Holy Spirit intervened, opening his eyes and revealing the truth of his peril," spoke an angel of extreme muscular build by the name of Gil-bore.

"Brothers, we could not afford to allow him to be taken. I have been informed from my superiors that there are important tasks and missions for Micah to perform. But even so, if Micah would not have repented and submitted himself to the Holy Spirit and called out for help, by now he would have been a byword and a castaway," Leb'abreck said.

"Comrades, we must not become relaxed in our mission. Even as you are aware that the battles are becoming much more intense, and many more are the casualties, now than ever before, are those falling by the wayside who were once deeply in love with God. They were filled with His fire and glory. But now they are caught up in materialism, vain amusements, and earthly pleasures. Surely this is the beginning of the end that was prophesied of by our Master in His earthly ministry," said Sawkal.

Nay-fo entered once again into the conversation. "In all of my journeys to earth, I have never experienced the vicious attacks as they are now. I agree with you, Sawkal. This must surely be the perilous days our Master had told His disciples about. There is such outright wickedness and rebellion. The whole world seems to have lost their minds and become like Sodom and Gomorrah. I do not understand why the Lord has not put an end to this perversion."

"It is because the Lord is waiting for the precious fruit of the earth, and until He receives the early and latter rain," Leb'abreck replied. "He has long patience for it. Then life will begin anew, for there will no longer be sin, death, or sorrow. But for a thousand years, there will be nothing but prosperity and total liberty," he concluded.

"Yes," said Tabeal. "All of creation is in travail waiting until the manifestation of the sons of God, the bride of Christ. What a glorious day that will be when we can finally lay down our weapons and once again enjoy all things even as it was before the terrible rebellion. But until then, we must fight with everything that our Master provides. For there are many out there just like Micah who are right on the brink of disaster."

"We must not fail," Leb'abreck responded, no matter the cost or the pain we experience. If our adversary wants to continue to fight up to the very end, then a fight they will have."

At this declaration, the small company of angels shouted their whole-hearted agreement.

Chapter 31
Moving On

When Micah woke up, the sun was shining through his bedroom window. It was 9:30 a.m. and he was late for work. He was still tired because he stayed up praying after the dream. All of his spiritual blindness was washed away in his acknowledgment and recognition of sin, like mud washes away in a heavy spring rain. He knew in his heart that he really did not love Stacy after all. It was a physical attraction with deep, emotional feelings. There was no question about it; it was not God's will for him to marry her. By yielding his mind and emotions to the wrong desires, he had gone down a path that would have hindered his ability to fulfill God's will for his life, maybe even destroy him. He also knew that though he was forgiven, he must still deal with the results of his sins. For the Scripture declares that "God is not mocked. For whatsoever a man sows that will he also reap."

It was going to be difficult to break off his relationship with Stacy. Even though he had repented, he was still very weak, and Stacy was bound and determined to have him. How could he get free from these wrong desires? How could he get back to where he belonged spiritually? It looked so far away that it was discouraging. *What did Pastor Ray say about moving on with God?* Micah asked himself. Then in his mind he heard his pastor saying, *Step-by-step, just put one spiritual foot in front of the other. Whatever you do, don't ever run away from God, but run to Him. The conviction of God is not your enemy but a divine umbrella to save your soul. Run into it. Stay in it, live there.*

As Micah meditated upon the pastor's words, the phone rang. Micah stood still, listening to it ring, but he could not bring himself to answer it. What would he do or say if it was Stacy? After about ten rings the phone was quiet. He walked over to the phone, picked it up, and called the office of the factory where he worked to let them know he wouldn't be coming in.

The rest of the day he stayed in an attitude of prayer and read Scripture. A verse that really spoke to him was the one that said that God would not let you be tempted above what you are able and that the Lord would make a way of escape. By late afternoon, Micah had come to a firm belief that He knew what God wanted him to do. It was drastic, but it was going to have to take something drastic to get out of the rut he was in. He sat down at his little kitchenette table and wrote a letter.

Dear Stacy,

this is one of the hardest letters I have ever had to write. By the time you receive this, I will be gone. I do not know where I'm going. All I know is that I missed God's will by getting involved with you. It's not your fault, so please do not blame yourself. Please forgive me if I have hurt you deeply, but the call of God upon my life is too strong for me to ignore. God must be first in my life. I know that I would not make the kind of husband you need. I also believe that I am in the will of God, and that this is the best thing to do for you and for me. I'm praying for you.

Love in Christ,

Micah

P.S. God has the perfect man for you, just be patient.

Micah folded the letter, stuffed it into a white envelope, sealed it, and wrote Stacy's address on it. He pulled out his old military duffel bag and began to pack it. He filled it only with those items that were absolutely necessary and could be carried on his motorcycle. He packed the remaining clothes and belongings in some boxes the landlord had left in a crawl space in the ceiling.

By the end of the day, he had already made the phone calls and arrangements that were necessary in order to fulfill his responsibilities before he moved. It's amazing the favor that the Lord granted him. Even though he should have given a two-week notice at his work place, his employer told him that they were going to have to lay him off anyway because work was so slow. Also, because it was at the end of the month, his landlord said that he would not require him to pay the next month's rent. In addition, Micah didn't have to move any furniture because he had rented a furnished apartment.

The next morning, Micah went to the local outdoors outlet and bought a small one-man tent and a compact goose-down sleeping bag. He also stopped by the post office to pick up his mail and to fill out change of address cards for the utility companies and other businesses he dealt with. Lester had agreed to receive his mail until he settled down. The last thing he mailed was his letter to Stacy.

By early afternoon, he arrived back at the apartment. Through part of the day he finished the little things that were still left undone, including cleaning the apartment from top to bottom.

Some of the brothers Micah had led to the Lord came over late in the afternoon to help him finish cleaning up and to pick up his belongings that had been packed in boxes. They stayed for a while and prayed with Micah. They all agreed for God's protection and guidance. He shared with them about how he had missed God, and why he had to do what he was doing in order to go on in the Lord. Micah hugged each one goodbye: Lester, Bobby, Willy Wine, Larry, and Tee Jay. Micah had many other friends in the Lord, too, but these were special brothers whom he had grown close to. The chief of police was also there to say goodbye. He was extremely grateful to Micah for witnessing to him because God had restored his marriage and family.

The rest of the day Micah worked on his motorcycle. He changed his oil, the air filter, checked the tire pressure, and adjusted the brakes. The bike was about ten years old and was in good shape. It was one of a new line of motorcycles that Harley Davidson had come out with in order to keep up with foreign competition. It had the mean-machine look, with a built-in global location LCD screen, a digital DAC player with digital/audio technology, extreme sound quality, and high-intensity fog lights. It was one fast, sleek machine, and Micah had just made his last payment a month earlier.

When everything had met his approval, Micah went back into his apartment. The phone was disconnected, so he had not gotten any phone calls that night. He wasn't surprised that Stacy had not showed up at his door. She had told him that on Monday she was going to go to her mother's parent's house for a couple of days. She was joining her mother there, and her father was going to have to leave to go back to work.

For the first time in a number of months, Micah slept easily. The next morning, he woke up extremely early and crawled out of his sleeping bag, which he had slept in on the now stripped-down bed. After dressing and getting ready, he walked through the apartment to make sure everything was done. He picked up his sleeping bag, the packed one-man tent, and a small duffel bag of clothes and walked out the front door, locking it as he left.

As he stepped out on the porch, the sun was just beginning to peak over the eastern horizon. It was going to be a beautiful and glorious day. He walked off the porch around to the side of the building where he kept his bike in his designated carport. He strapped the tent and duffel bag to the passenger backrest, leaving the sleeping bag for last so he could use it to rest his back against. He placed the key in its ignition, swung his foot over the bike, and straddled it.

Micah sat there for a while, excitement bubbling inside of him. Once again, he felt the presence of the Lord in his life. Something significant was taking place. A chapter in his life had just closed and another one was just about to open.

As he sat there, a squirrel ran across the blacktop toward a tree with a mouth full of acorns. He heard birds singing somewhere in the distance. A robin was on the lawn looking for worms.

Well, I might as well start this journey the right way, Micah said to himself as he bowed his head to pray. *Father God, thank you for this day and for another chance*. For a brief period Micah was overwhelmed with the presence of the Lord as he communicated his love with human words to God. He knew that without the divine intervention of God, it would have all been over for him. *Lord, lead me in the path of righteousness for Your name's sake. And I thank You for Your angels that protect me in all ways. Amen.*

He reached over on his right side, pulled the starting pedal out, put his foot on it, and kicked down hard. The engine roared to life with a loud rumble. He could have used the electric starter, but he preferred the old method. He flicked the car into first gear with his left foot, turned the accelerator with his right hand, released the clutch, and pulled away from the curb.

The sun was shining on his back as he headed west. Behind him was the past that included many glorious experiences and victories, but it also included shameful sins and defeat. Before him lay an endless horizon where all things are possible to those who believe.

Chapter 32
Punishment

A whip snapped with sharpness and clarity of sound. Demons laughed and mocked their companion out loud. Belee was strapped to an ugly gnarled post. He screamed with agony and pleaded unceasingly to a black, grotesque figure that stood over him wielding a long, sleek whip in his hand. The air smelled like there was a rotting corpse in the vicinity. The ruling spirit drew back his arm, raised the whip, and a streak went whistling through the air, hitting Belee squarely on the back as it wrapped itself around his body. The ruling spirit pulled the whip back, ripping ugly copper skin and digging a furrow through his back.

Terrible, ear-piercing screams emanated from the tortured spirit. "No...not again...no please. I abjure you in the name of satan, don't. It wasn't my fault. The angels of the Almighty stepped in. We couldn't stop them. The believer called upon them for help."

Once again the lash of the whip came down on his back. Pain flooded him, bringing nausea and momentary darkness. Screams once more filled the cavern.

"I am going to make an example of you," growled a voice that sounded like steel ripping. "You have failed me once again. One too many times." Again the whip came down, whistling as it slashed through the air.

When Belee recovered from the last stroke, he begged for mercy. "But, your wickedness, I couldn't control his free will. Everything was set up just right. Lust was burning in his mind like a red-hot poker. The female human was begging for him to partake of the forbidden fruit. I was there, your wickedness, with my horde. The angels stood off at a distance, and right in the midst of our highest expectations, he turned his heart to our adversary, asking for help. A bolt of lightning streaked out

153

of the heavenlies, hitting us with its full force. Many of my horde were scorched and burned. Only a small number of us were able to regroup and attack Micah once again. But it was too late. Our stronghold over him was broken."

"I don't want to hear your excuses," screamed the disgruntled voice of his superior. The whip came down again, streaking across his face and chest. He cried out with pain and agony. Cruel laughter and mockery filtered throughout the darkness of the evil realm as punishment was delved out.

As Micah drove down the highway, a small band of angels surrounded him. Tabeal and Tsaphah were in front of him; Nay-fo and Saw-on were in the rear, Gil-bore and Sawkal were to the left and to the right. Leb'abreck was immediately above him looking in every direction. Even though Micah was cruising at sixty-five miles per hour, it did not seem in the least to be putting pressures upon the angelic bodyguard. They had their swords drawn and their eyes alert, ready for an attack of the enemy if he would show his face.

Micah rounded a sharp corner, leaning into the curve. There were high banks with trees on both sides. Just as Micah was at the sharpest point, he saw a flash off to his left. Faster than he could possibly react, a large deer, a buck, leaped in front of him. Micah knew instantly that it was too late. He was going to hit the leaping deer. At sixty-five miles per hour, he knew their bodies would be tangled together in blood, guts, skin, and hide.

The hoofs of the deer were only inches from Micah's head as it leapt into the air. And then, at the very last possible moment, the deer seemed to be lifted higher into the air, right over Micah's head and his bike. The deer landed on the other side of the road and continued to run.

Gil-bore, though invisible to the naked eye of a mortal, had seen a number of demons frightening the deer in the woods and had seen it take off like a scared rabbit. As it leapt toward Micah's head, Gil-bore was there to lift the deer up and over Micah's head safely to the other side of the road. Sawkal went in pursuit of the devilish spirits who had frightened the deer in order to kill Micah. When he caught up with them, they would pay dearly for their mischief.

Micah was totally overcome with praise. He knew it had to be a divine intervention. There was no way he could not have collided with the deer. He was so overjoyed that, without thinking, he lifted both of his hands off of the handlebars. Leb'abreck swept down from above, grabbed the handles, and steered the cycle down the road as Micah was engrossed in worship.

Chapter 33
On the Road

It was late in the afternoon, and the sun was shining brightly on Micah's face. It had been two days since he had left his hometown in Delaware. He was headed northwest, not really having any destination in mind. He was just going by the leading in his heart. He felt like Abraham when God had called him out of the city of the Chaldeans to a land he did not know. It was a strange feeling to be free from all natural ties and to have God as the only source of security. Where he would end up, only God knew. But that was all right, for if God was with Micah, who could be against him?

The sun was setting as he pulled into a campground. He went into the office and paid for a campsite for one night. Back outside he drove his bike around the campgrounds until he found himself a quiet, secluded spot. It was perfect; it even had large pine trees perched upon a rolling hillside looking down upon him.

After he set up his tent and rolled out his sleeping bag, he built a small fire in the ground barrier that was provided for campfires. Then he took out military field utensils and cooked himself a can of pork and beans with a pack of hot dogs that he had just purchased at the camp store. When he was done and had cleaned up from the meal, he sat down next to the fire with his Bible. As he read it, he found himself totally immersed. It was profound and life changing. Before he gave his heart to the Lord, he had read the Bible some, but it really did not make a lot of sense. But now that he knew God, the Scriptures seemed to jump off the pages at him. It was like a drink of fresh spring water in a dry and thirsty land. It reminded him of his grandma's homemade bread when it was fresh from the oven with a big slab of farm-churned butter melting in the middle of a thick-cut slice. The taste was indescribable. "That is what it is," Micah said to himself. "It's manna from heaven."

By the time he put down the Bible, the sun had set in the west. The fire was burning low, and Micah could hear a whippoorwill in the woods. As he gazed up, the stars already were shining brightly. He was overcome with the vastness of it all. To think that God, by the hands of Jesus, had created it all. Looking down upon him from above was his future, as it would be for all true believers who loved the Lord sincerely with all of their heart. He knew that if he and others like him would be faithful over the little things that were placed in their hands upon this earth, they would rule and reign with Christ over all creation. Those meditations flowed through Micah's heart as he looked at the promises in God's Word. The promises were a reality in Micah's heart. He lived for the day when he could hear the heavenly Father say, "Well done, thou good and faithful servant, enter into the joy of thy salvation." Surely the sufferings of this present world, the sacrifices he had made and would have to make, the persecutions he would go through, and the pains he would have to endure, were not to be compared with the glory that would be revealed in Christ.

Micah arose from the ground, went into his tent and crawled into the sleeping bag. Just before he fell asleep, he mumbled a prayer. "Lord, I only have one life to live in this world, and I am going to live it for You. Jesus, You gave Your all for me, and that is the least I can do for You."

That night he dreamed a dream. An angel of the Lord stood before him. As the angel spoke, the whole earth shook and the mountains fled from his presence. The angel called him by name. "Micah, servant of the Most High." In the dream, Micah fell to his face before this mighty creature. "Stand to your feet, for I am only a ministering angel sent forth to help you in your mission. The Lord God Almighty has sent me with a message. The Lord has placed His Spirit upon you and anointed you to declare the words of life unto the inhabitants of the lands where unto He shall send you. For you shall stand before peoples of different nations. Before kings and dignitaries you will declare the truths of His Word."

"But who am I, that the Lord Most High would choose such as me? For I am but a worm and a man of unclean lips. I do not deserve to be called a son of God. I have failed the Lord miserably," Micah cried out, tears flowing down his face.

"Do not fear, Micah, for the Lord has blotted out your transgressions and nailed them to His cross. He has placed upon you the robe of His righteousness and the crown of His authority," the angel replied.

In the dream, Micah saw a brilliant white and glistening robe upon him. A crown sat upon his head. Jewels of many sizes, types, and colors sparkled in its framework. Under the robe was a gown that gleamed like the flash of a lightning bolt. As Micah looked upon those garments gracing his body, he heard a voice, not the voice of an angel anymore, but another voice. Immediately he knew in his heart who it was. It was the voice of his Master, the Lamb of God slain before the foundations of the world, the King of kings, and the Lord of lords. It was Jesus of Nazareth.

"Go, Micah, in My name, by My grace, strength, and power. Tell My children who they are in Me, for many have not had a revelation that I live in them. Many are destroyed for a lack of knowledge, and because they have rejected knowledge, I will have to reject them unless they repent."

At that very moment, it was as if scales fell off of Micah's eyes. He was a loser, a nobody, a low-life, a failure in and by himself. But through the life of Christ, he was a child of the King. Micah was more than a conqueror, and an overcomer. He was a priest and a king, an ambassador of God Almighty, and a messenger sent to a lost and dying world. In Christ, he was who God's Word declared him to be. In Christ, he could overcome the world, the flesh, and the devil. Even as it was proclaimed in the Word, so it was true for all who would believe.

Micah opened his eyes. Sunshine cast a red hue upon him as it filtered through the walls of the tent. He crawled out of the sleeping bag, opened the tent flap and was greeted by a slight warm breeze. He stepped out of the tent and straightened his back. It was a new day, a new beginning, with a brighter tomorrow. Yes, he would answer the call of God. It did not matter where it took him, and it did not matter what it cost. Micah would not be disobedient to this vision.

About the Author

Dr. Michael H. Yeager is a motivated speaker who would love to come and minister to your church or group. You can reach him through the following:

Address:
Jesus is Lord ministries international
3425 Chambersburg Rd.
Biglerville, Pennsylvania 17307

Phone: 1-800-555-4575

Websites:
www.docyeager.org
www.wordbroadcast.org
www.hellsreal.com

Horrors of Hell, Splendors of Heaven
by Dr. Michael Yeager
$15.00
ISBN: 978-0-9825775-9-2

When you read the true story of Dr. Michael Yeager's encounter with the afterlife, you too will realize the indescribable depth of the horrors of hell, and the unimaginable splendors of heaven. Fall into the gut-wrenching realms of the damned, enter into the divine gates of heaven, and be escorted by an angel into an amazing dimension of beauty and nature. End your journey upon the sea of glass before the thunder and lightning of God's throne. Along the way, you will discover answers to your deepest questions about the afterlife. As you take the journey to hell, heaven, and back, the revelations you receive will be eternal.